MW00472885

Bible Promises
to Treasure
for Business Professionals

Inspiring

words

for every

occasion

BROADMAN
&HOLMAN
PUBLISHERS

Nashville, Tennessee

Bible Promises
to Treasure
for Business Professionals

Bible Promises to Treasure for Business Professionals
©1998 Broadman & Holman Publishers,
Nashville, Tennessee
All rights reserved
Printed in Belgium

ISBN 0-8054-9333-6

Dewey Decimal Classification: 242.68
Subject Heading: BUSINESS PEOPLE. RELIGIOUS LIFE

******

A note on the sources of quotations. When possible I have supplied at least the book name from which contemporary quotes have come. Yet even this is often impossible, since many came from my "journal of jottings" over many years. Also, if a quote is from a person who lived longer than fifty or so years ago, I've made no attempt to cite the source. Such quotations are usually available in any standard book of quotes.

******

Library of Congress Cataloging-in-Publication Data
Bible promises to treasure for business professionals : inspiring
   words for every occasion / compiled by Gary Wilde.
      p. cm.
   Includes bibliographical references.
   ISBN 0-8054-9333-6
   1. Businesspeople—Religious life. 2. Christian life—
Quotations maxims, etc.   I. Wilde, Gary
BV4596.B8B54   1999
242'.68—dc21   98–34850
                                                                CIP

1 2 3 4 5 6 02 01 00 99 98

Contents

Introduction

I remember as a child singing often at church: "Standing on the Promises of God." Or maybe it was mostly the adults who were singing; but I was standing next to them—my parents and all the others. I recall those faithful people joyfully reciting words they must surely have known by heart . . .

> **When the howling storms
> of doubt and fear assail,
> By the living Word of God I shall prevail,
> Standing on the promises of God.**

For years Downey Church, in sunny central Florida, had preached and taught the promises *of God and believed in His goodness. From the beginning—when the church building was a small tin-roofed, A-frame at the east end of a dirt road on the outskirts of Orlando—people would gather to stand on the immutable promises. Under the shiny tin roof, standing on the sandy-wooden floorboards, they melded their voices to the tunes of the upright piano and recalled God's goodness. Today, as the church there grows and thrives—now there is also a school and gymnasium—I can only attribute its vibrant life to a love of God's promises and the recognition that without the pledges that flow from the mouth of God, there is no church, no music, and no reason for either.*

The promises of God have always been the bedrock of Christian faith; for without God's sacred covenants with us, we cannot survive. In times of joy or heartache, in all our ups and downs, we keep coming back to that source of our life: the motivation for all our doing and the reason for our existence. It is the message of God's mighty assurances: this life is not all there is, He will always be with us while we are here, and He will take us to be with Him someday. Yes, we do have priceless promises to keep close to our hearts!

My hope for you as you delve into this scriptural treasure chest is that you will grow deeper in love with the One who has spoken as no other ever could. With so many influences bombarding our minds each moment of the day, what could be better than to set aside a few moments of quiet to hear the still, small voice that constantly invites us into warm fellowship? We'll be richly rewarded if we truly listen to what that voice is saying. His words convey blessing and guidance, wisdom and warning, life for now and life everlasting. What incomparable grace!

Gary Wilde
Oviedo, Florida, 1998

One

Working So Hard...But What's the Point?

Long ago the wisest man on earth realized that he could never find complete fulfillment in this life—not in learning, not in pleasure, and not even in great accomplishments through hard work. In all of his depression over this, Solomon nevertheless maintained a rock-solid conviction that we can still enjoy our life and work here on earth if we will simply

acknowledge our duty to God as the key to everything. Have you come to this blessed realization yet?

Bored with Work?

Many workers in the modern marketplace feel increasingly bored with their jobs and with life. This is the subtext of all the glitzy beer, hamburger, and travel commercials that show hardworking laborers building America and solving its problems. They portray the work place not as it is but as we wish it could be—an engrossing, challenging, even uplifting human drama in which each of us performs our strategic role and fulfills a personal mission. Instead, for many work is "just a job." Its value begins and ends with a paycheck.

—Doug Sherman and William Hendricks[1]

What profit hath a man of all his labour which he taketh under the sun?

—*Ecclesiastes 1:3*

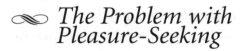 The Vanity of Life Apart from God

Then came the word of the LORD by Haggai the prophet, saying,

Is it time for you, O ye, to dwell in your ceiled houses, and this house [the Temple] lie waste?

Now therefore thus saith the LORD of hosts; Consider your ways.

Ye have sown much, and bring in little; ye eat, but ye have not enough; ye drink, but ye are not filled with drink; ye clothe you, but there is none warm; and he that earneth wages earneth wages to put it into a bag with holes.

Thus saith the LORD of hosts; Consider your ways.

—Haggai 1:3–7

The Problem with Pleasure-Seeking

I said in mine heart, Go to now, I will prove thee with mirth, therefore enjoy pleasure: and, behold, this also is vanity.

I said of laughter, It is mad: and of mirth, What doeth it?

I sought in mine heart to give myself unto wine, yet acquainting mine heart with wisdom; and to lay hold on folly, till I might see what was that good for the sons of men, which they should do under the heaven all the days of their life.

I made me great works; I builded me houses; I planted me vineyards:

I made me gardens and orchards, and I planted trees in them of all kind of fruits:

I made me pools of water, to water therewith the wood that bringeth forth trees:

I got me servants and maidens, and had servants born in my house; also I had great possessions of great and small cattle above all that were in Jerusalem before me:

I gathered me also silver and gold, and the peculiar treasure of kings and of the provinces: I gat me men singers and women singers, and the delights of the sons of men, as musical instruments, and that of all sorts.

So I was great, and increased more than all that were before me in Jerusalem: also my wisdom remained with me.

And whatsoever mine eyes desired I kept not from them, I withheld not my heart from any joy; for my heart rejoiced in all my labour: and this was my portion of all my labour.

Then I looked on all the works that my hands had wrought, and on the labour that I had laboured to do: and, behold, all was vanity and vexation of spirit, and there was no profit under the sun.

—*Ecclesiastes 2:1–11*

And he said, A certain man had two sons:

And the younger of them said to his father, Father, give me the portion of goods that falleth to me. And he divided unto them his living.

And not many days after the younger son gathered all together, and took his journey into a far country, and there wasted his substance with riotous living.

And when he had spent all, there arose a mighty famine in that land; and he began to be in want.

And he went and joined himself to a citizen of that country; and he sent him into his fields to feed swine.

And he would fain have filled his belly with the husks that the swine did eat: and no man gave unto him.

And when he came to himself, he said, How many hired servants of my father's have bread enough and to spare, and I perish with hunger!

—Luke 15:11–17

∾ The Prevalance of Injustice

And moreover I saw under the sun the place of judgment, that wickedness was there; and the place of righteousness, that iniquity was there.

I said in mine heart, God shall judge the righteous and the wicked: for there is a time there for every purpose and for every work.

I said in mine heart concerning the estate of the sons of men, that God might manifest them, and that they might see that they themselves are beasts.

For that which befalleth the sons of men befalleth beasts; even one thing befalleth them: as the one dieth, so dieth the other; yea, they have all one breath; so that a man hath no preeminence above a beast: for all is vanity.

All go unto one place; all are of the dust, and all turn to dust again.

Who knoweth the spirit of man that goeth upward, and the spirit of the beast that goeth downward to the earth?

—*Ecclesiastes 3:16–21*

There were present at that season some that told him of the Galilaeans, whose blood Pilate had mingled with their sacrifices.

And Jesus answering said unto them, Suppose ye that these Galilaeans were sinners above all the Galilaeans, because they suffered such things?

I tell you, Nay: but, except ye repent, ye shall all likewise perish.

Or those eighteen, upon whom the tower in Siloam fell, and slew them, think ye that they were sinners above all men that dwelt in Jerusalem?

—*Luke 13:1–4*

For he maketh his sun to rise on the evil and on the good, and sendeth rain on the just and on the unjust.

—*Matthew 5:45*

❧ *The Short-Lived Joy of Accomplishment*

If thou seest the oppression of the poor, and violent perverting of judgment and justice in a province, marvel not at the matter: for he that is higher than the highest regardeth; and there be higher than they.

Moreover the profit of the earth is for all: the king himself is served by the field.

He that loveth silver shall not be satisfied with silver; nor he that loveth abundance with increase: this is also vanity.

When goods increase, they are increased that eat them: and what good is there to the owners thereof, saving the beholding of them with their eyes?

The sleep of a labouring man is sweet, whether he eat little or much: but the abundance of the rich will not suffer him to sleep.

There is a sore evil which I have seen under the sun, namely, riches kept for the owners thereof to their hurt.

But those riches perish by evil travail: and he begetteth a son, and there is nothing in his hand.

As he came forth of his mother's womb, naked shall he return to go as he came, and shall take nothing of his labour, which he may carry away in his hand.

And this also is a sore evil, that in all points as he came, so shall he go: and what profit hath he that hath laboured for the wind?

All his days also he eateth in darkness, and he hath much sorrow and wrath with his sickness.

—*Ecclesiastes 5:8–17*

∾ *Anyway, You Can't Take It with You!*

There is an evil which I have seen under the sun, and it is common among men:

A man to whom God hath given riches, wealth, and honour, so that he wanteth nothing for his soul of all that he desireth, yet God giveth him not power to eat thereof, but a stranger eateth it: this is vanity, and it is an evil disease.

If a man beget an hundred children, and live many years, so that the days of his years be many, and his soul be not filled with good, and also that he have no burial; I say, that an untimely birth is better than he.

For he cometh in with vanity, and departeth in darkness, and his name shall be covered with darkness.

Moreover he hath not seen the sun, nor known any thing: this hath more rest than the other.

Yea, though he live a thousand years twice told, yet hath he seen no good: do not all go to one place?

—*Ecclesiastes 6:1–6*

But a certain man named Ananias, with Sapphira his wife, sold a possession,

And kept back part of the price, his wife also being privy to it, and brought a certain part, and laid it at the apostles' feet.

But Peter said, Ananias, why hath Satan filled thine heart to lie to the Holy Ghost, and to keep back part of the price of the land?

Whiles it remained, was it not thine own? and after it was sold, was it not in thine own power? why hast thou conceived this thing in thine heart? thou hast not lied unto men, but unto God.

And Ananias hearing these words fell down, and gave up the ghost: and great fear came on all them that heard these things.

And the young men arose, wound him up, and carried him out, and buried him.

And it was about the space of three hours after, when his wife, not knowing what was done, came in.

And Peter answered unto her, Tell me whether ye sold the land for so much? And she said, Yea, for so much.

Then Peter said unto her, How is it that ye have agreed together to tempt the Spirit of the Lord? behold, the feet of them which have buried thy husband are at the door, and shall carry thee out.

—*Acts 5:1–9*

❧ *Might As Well Enjoy All that God Gives*

To every thing there is a season, and a time to every purpose under the heaven:

A time to be born, and a time to die; a time to plant, and a time to pluck up that which is planted;

A time to kill, and a time to heal; a time to break down, and a time to build up;

A time to weep, and a time to laugh; a time to mourn, and a time to dance;

A time to cast away stones, and a time to gather stones together; a time to embrace, and a time to refrain from embracing;

A time to get, and a time to lose; a time to keep, and a time to cast away;

A time to rend, and a time to sew; a time to keep silence, and a time to speak;

A time to love, and a time to hate; a time of war, and a time of peace.

—*Ecclesiastes 3:1–8*

Go thy way, eat thy bread with joy, and drink thy wine with a merry heart; for God now accepteth thy works.

Let thy garments be always white; and let thy head lack no ointment.

Live joyfully with the wife whom thou lovest all the days of the life of thy vanity, which he hath given thee under the sun, all the days of thy vanity: for that is thy portion in this life, and in thy labour which thou takest under the sun.

Whatsoever thy hand findeth to do, do it with thy might; for there is no work, nor device, nor knowledge, nor wisdom, in the grave, whither thou goest.

—Ecclesiastes 9:7–10

The LORD is my shepherd; I shall not want.

He maketh me to lie down in green pastures: he leadeth me beside the still waters.

—Psalm 23:1–2

. . . But Remember Why You Are Here

This is the longing of all mankind—to have security, to know where one's place is. God created man and then he created a place for him, the Garden of Eden. When man lost God he lost at the same time his place. Since then, the longing for a place where he belongs, where he feels at home, is in the heart of every human being. In light of this, Jesus' promise "to prepare a place" for us is filled with new meaning. Those who have found him have found their place.

—*Walter Trobisch*[2]

Because the preacher was wise, he still taught the people knowledge; yea, he gave good heed, and sought out, and set in order many proverbs.

The preacher sought to find out acceptable words: and that which was written was upright, even words of truth.

The words of the wise are as goads, and as nails fastened by the masters of assemblies, which are given from one shepherd.

And further, by these, my son, be admonished: of making many books there is no end; and much study is a weariness of the flesh.

Let us hear the conclusion of the whole matter: Fear God, and keep his commandments: for this is the whole duty of man.

For God shall bring every work into judgment, with every secret thing, whether it be good, or whether it be evil.

—*Ecclesiastes 12:9–14*

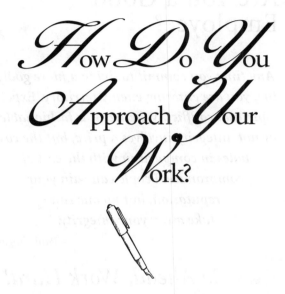

Two

How Do You Approach Your Work?

It's possible to get the job done without paying much attention to the process involved. However, that's not the best way to approach our tasks. After all, the end never justifies the means. We could do good work with a mean spirit, for instance. Yet our Lord is much more concerned with who we are becoming than with what we are accomplishing.

Are You a Good Employee?

Any time you commit to living a more godly life, you are entering enemy territory. Expect spiritual conflict. Whether it is fashionable or not, integrity involves a price, but the cost pales in comparison with the cost of compromise. People can ruin your reputation, but no one can take away your integrity.

—*Paul Kroger[1]*

∞ *Go Ahead, Work Hard!*

The sleep of a labouring man is sweet, whether he eat little or much.

—*Ecclesiastes 5:12*

In the sweat of thy face shalt thou eat bread, till thou return unto the ground; for out of it wast thou taken: for dust thou art, and unto dust shalt thou return.

—*Genesis 3:19*

Six days shalt thou labour, and do all thy work:

But the seventh day is the sabbath of the LORD thy God: in it thou shalt not do any work, thou, nor thy son, nor thy daughter, thy manservant, nor thy maidservant, nor thy cattle, nor thy stranger that is within thy gates:

For in six days the LORD made heaven and earth, the sea, and all that in them is, and rested the seventh day: wherefore the LORD blessed the sabbath day, and hallowed it.

—Exodus 20:9–11

Now to him that worketh is the reward not reckoned of grace, but of debt.

—Romans 4:4

For the scripture saith, Thou shalt not muzzle the ox that treadeth out the corn. And, The labourer is worthy of his reward.

—1 Timothy 5:18

∾ *Display Initiative*

Go to the ant, thou sluggard; consider her ways, and be wise:

Which having no guide, overseer, or ruler,

Provideth her meat in the summer, and gathereth her food in the harvest.

How long wilt thou sleep, O sluggard? when wilt thou arise out of thy sleep?

Yet a little sleep, a little slumber, a little folding of the hands to sleep:

So shall thy poverty come as one that travelleth, and thy want as an armed man.

—Proverbs 6:6–11

He becometh poor that dealeth with a slack hand: but the hand of the diligent maketh rich.

He that gathereth in summer is a wise son: but he that sleepeth in harvest is a son that causeth shame. . . .

As vinegar to the teeth, and as smoke to the eyes, so is the sluggard to them that send him.

—Proverbs 10:4–5, 26

He that is despised, and hath a servant, is better than he that honoureth himself, and lacketh bread. . . .

The hand of the diligent shall bear rule: but the slothful shall be under tribute. . . .

The slothful man roasteth not that which he took in hunting: but the substance of a diligent man is precious.

—*Proverbs 12:9, 24, 27*

Slothfulness casteth into a deep sleep; and an idle soul shall suffer hunger. . . .

A slothful man hideth his hand in his bosom, and will not so much as bring it to his mouth again.

—*Proverbs 19:15, 24*

The sluggard will not plow by reason of the cold; therefore shall he beg in harvest, and have nothing. . . .

Love not sleep, lest thou come to poverty; open thine eyes, and thou shalt be satisfied with bread.

—*Proverbs 20:4, 13*

The desire of the slothful killeth him; for his hands refuse to labour.

He coveteth greedily all the day long: but the righteous giveth and spareth not.

—*Proverbs 21:25–26*

Follow the Example of Good Workers

It's no trick to make a lot of money, if all you want to do is make a lot of money.

—*Orson Welles[2]*

∞ *Joseph: A Thoroughly Trustworthy Steward*

And the LORD was with Joseph, and he was a prosperous man; and he was in the house of his master the Egyptian.

And his master saw that the LORD was with him, and that the LORD made all that he did to prosper in his hand.

And Joseph found grace in his sight, and he served him: and he made him overseer over his house, and all that he had he put into his hand.

And it came to pass from the time that he had made him overseer in his house, and over all that he had, that the LORD blessed the Egyptian's house for Joseph's sake; and the blessing of the LORD was upon all that he had in the house, and in the field.

And he left all that he had in Joseph's hand; and he knew not ought he had, save the bread which he did eat. And Joseph was a goodly person, and well favoured.

And it came to pass after these things, that his master's wife cast her eyes upon Joseph; and she said, Lie with me.

But he refused, and said unto his master's wife, Behold, my master wotteth not what is with me in the house, and he hath committed all that he hath to my hand;

There is none greater in this house than I; neither hath he kept back any thing from me but thee, because thou art his wife: how then can I do this great wickedness, and sin against God?

—*Genesis 39:2–9*

And [God] delivered him out of all his afflictions, and gave him favour and wisdom in the sight of Pharaoh king of Egypt; and he made him governor over Egypt and all his house.

—*Acts 7:10*

∞ *Elisha: A Completely Loyal Colleague*

And it came to pass, when the LORD would take up Elijah into heaven by a whirlwind, that Elijah went with Elisha from Gilgal.

And Elijah said unto Elisha, Tarry here, I pray thee; for the LORD hath sent me to Beth–el. And Elisha said unto him, As the LORD liveth, and as thy soul liveth, I will not leave thee. So they went down to Beth–el.

And the sons of the prophets that were at Beth–el came forth to Elisha, and said unto him, Knowest thou that the LORD will take away thy master from thy head to day? And he said, Yea, I know it; hold ye your peace.

And Elijah said unto him, Elisha, tarry here, I pray thee; for the LORD hath sent me to Jericho. And he said, As the LORD liveth, and as thy soul liveth, I will not leave thee. So they came to Jericho.

And the sons of the prophets that were at Jericho came to Elisha, and said unto him, Knowest thou that the LORD will take away thy master from thy head to day? And he answered, Yea, I know it; hold ye your peace.

And Elijah said unto him, Tarry, I pray thee, here; for the LORD hath sent me to Jordan. And he said, As the LORD liveth, and as thy soul liveth, I will not leave thee. And they two went on.

—*2 Kings 2:1–6*

∞ *The Servant of Abigail: A Trusted Confidant*

But one of the young men told Abigail, Nabal's wife, saying, Behold, David sent messengers out of the wilderness to salute our master; and he railed on them.

But the men were very good unto us, and we were not hurt, neither missed we any thing, as long as we were conversant with them, when we were in the fields:

They were a wall unto us both by night and day, all the while we were with them keeping the sheep.

Now therefore know and consider what thou wilt do; for evil is determined against our master, and against all his household: for he is such a son of Belial, that a man cannot speak to him.

—1 Samuel 25:14–17

∞ *Ziba: A Knowledgeable Helper*

And David said, Is there yet any that is left of the house of Saul, that I may shew him kindness for Jonathan's sake?

And there was of the house of Saul a servant whose name was Ziba. And when they had called him unto David, the king said unto him, Art thou Ziba? And he said, Thy servant is he.

And the king said, Is there not yet any of the house of Saul, that I may shew the kindness of God unto him? And Ziba said unto the king, Jonathan hath yet a son, which is lame on his feet.

And the king said unto him, Where is he? And Ziba said unto the king, Behold, he is in the house of Machir, the son of Ammiel, in Lo–debar.

Then king David sent, and fetched him out of the house of Machir, the son of Ammiel, from Lo–debar.

Now when Mephibosheth, the son of Jonathan, the son of Saul, was come unto David, he fell on his face, and did reverence. And David said, Mephibosheth. And he answered, Behold thy servant!

And David said unto him, Fear not: for I will surely shew thee kindness for Jonathan thy father's sake, and will restore thee all the land of Saul thy father; and thou shalt eat bread at my table continually.

And he bowed himself, and said, What is thy servant, that thou shouldest look upon such a dead dog as I am?

Then the king called to Ziba, Saul's servant and said unto him, I have given unto thy master's son all that pertained to Saul and to all his house.

Thou therefore, and thy sons, and thy servants, shall till the land for him, and thou shalt bring in the fruits, that thy master's son may have food to eat: but Mephibosheth thy master's son shall eat bread alway at my table. Now Ziba had fifteen sons and twenty servants.

Then said Ziba unto the king, According to all that my lord the king hath commanded his servant, so shall thy servant do. As for Mephibosheth, said the king, he shall eat at my table, as one of the king's sons.

And Mephibosheth had a young son, whose name was Micha. And all that dwelt in the house of Ziba were servants unto Mephibosheth.

So Mephibosheth dwelt in Jerusalem: for he did eat continually at the king's table; and was lame on both his feet.

—2 Samuel 9

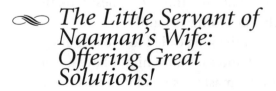

The Little Servant of Naaman's Wife: Offering Great Solutions!

And the Syrians had gone out by companies, and had brought away captive out of the land of Israel a little maid; and she waited on Naaman's wife.

And she said unto her mistress, Would God my lord were with the prophet that is in Samaria! for he would recover him of his leprosy.

And one went in, and told his lord, saying, Thus and thus said the maid that is of the land of Israel.

And the king of Syria said, Go to, go, and I will send a letter unto the king of Israel. And he departed, and took with him ten talents of silver, and six thousand pieces of gold, and ten changes of raiment.

And he brought the letter to the king of Israel, saying, Now when this letter is come unto thee, behold, I have therewith sent Naaman my servant to thee, that thou mayest recover him of his leprosy.

And it came to pass, when the king of Israel had read the letter, that he rent his clothes, and said, Am I God, to kill and to make alive, that this man doth send unto me to recover a man of his leprosy? wherefore consider, I pray you, and see how he seeketh a quarrel against me.

And it was so, when Elisha the man of God had heard that the king of Israel had rent his clothes, that he sent to the king, saying, Wherefore hast thou rent thy clothes? let him come now to me, and he shall know that there is a prophet in Israel.

So Naaman came with his horses and with his chariot, and stood at the door of the house of Elisha.

And Elisha sent a messenger unto him, saying, Go and wash in Jordan seven times, and thy flesh shall come again to thee, and thou shalt be clean.

But Naaman was wroth, and went away, and said, Behold, I thought, He will surely come out to me, and stand, and call on the name of the LORD his God, and strike his hand over the place, and recover the leper.

Are not Abana and Pharpar, rivers of Damascus, better than all the waters of Israel? may I not wash in them, and be clean? So he turned and went away in a rage.

And his servants came near, and spake unto him, and said, My father, if the prophet had bid thee do some great thing, wouldest thou not have done it? how much rather then, when he saith to thee, Wash, and be clean?

—*2 Kings 5:2–13*

Are You a Good Employer?

If at first you don't succeed, you may be at your level of incompetence already.

—*Laurence J. Peter*[3]

Woe unto him that buildeth his house by unrighteousness, and his chambers by wrong; that useth his neighbour's service without wages, and giveth him not for his work.

—*Jeremiah 22:13*

Thou shalt not oppress an hired servant that is poor and needy, whether he be of thy brethren, or of thy strangers that are in thy land within thy gates:

At his day thou shalt give him his hire, neither shall the sun go down upon it; for he is poor, and setteth his heart upon it: lest he cry against thee unto the LORD, and it be sin unto thee.

—*Deuteronomy 24:14–15*

If I did despise the cause of my manservant or of my maidservant, when they contended with me;

What then shall I do when God riseth up? and when he visiteth, what shall I answer him?

Did not he that made me in the womb make him? and did not one fashion us in the womb?

—*Job 31:13–15*

Use Your Authority in a Spirit of Servanthood

It is not enough merely to exist. It's not enough to say, "I'm earning enough to support my family, I do my work well. I'm a good father, husband, churchgoer."

*That's all very well. But you must do
something more. Seek always to do some
good, somewhere. Every man has to seek in
his own way to realize his true worth. You
must give some time to your fellow man.
Even if it's a little thing, do something for
those who need help, something for which
you get no pay but the privilege of doing it.
For remember, you don't live in a world all
your own. Your brothers are here too.*

—*Albert Schweitzer*[4]

[Jesus] riseth from supper, and laid aside
his garments; and took a towel, and girded
himself.

After that he poureth water into a basin,
and began to wash the disciples' feet, and to
wipe them with the towel wherewith he was
girded.

Then cometh he to Simon Peter: and
Peter saith unto him, Lord, dost thou wash
my feet?

Jesus answered and said unto him, What I
do thou knowest not now; but thou shalt
know hereafter.

Peter saith unto him, Thou shalt never wash my feet. Jesus answered him, If I wash thee not, thou hast no part with me.

Simon Peter saith unto him, Lord, not my feet only, but also my hands and my head.

Jesus saith to him, He that is washed needeth not save to wash his feet, but is clean every whit: and ye are clean, but not all.

For he knew who should betray him; therefore said he, Ye are not all clean.

So after he had washed their feet, and had taken his garments, and was set down again, he said unto them, Know ye what I have done to you?

Ye call me Master and Lord: and ye say well; for so I am.

If I then, your Lord and Master, have washed your feet; ye also ought to wash one another's feet.

For I have given you an example, that ye should do as I have done to you.

Verily, verily, I say unto you, The servant is not greater than his lord; neither he that is sent greater than he that sent him.

If ye know these things, happy are ye if ye do them.

—John 13:4–17

∾ Don't Be Cruel and Demanding . . .

He that oppresseth the poor to increase his riches, and he that giveth to the rich, shall surely come to want.

—Proverbs 22:16

And I will come near to you to judgment; and I will be a swift witness against the sorcerers, and against the adulterers, and against false swearers, and against those that oppress the hireling in his wages, the widow, and the fatherless, and that turn aside the stranger from his right, and fear not me, saith the LORD of hosts.

—Malachi 3:5

Behold, the hire of the labourers who have reaped down your fields, which is of you kept back by fraud, crieth: and the cries of them which have reaped are entered into the ears of the Lord of sabaoth.

—*James 5:4*

∾ *Be Kind and Supportive, Instead . . .*

And, behold, Boaz came from Bethlehem, and said unto the reapers, The LORD be with you. And they answered him, The LORD bless thee.

—*Ruth 2:4*

And a certain centurion's servant, who was dear unto him, was sick, and ready to die.

And when he heard of Jesus, he sent unto him the elders of the Jews, beseeching him that he would come and heal his servant.

And when they came to Jesus, they besought him instantly, saying, That he was worthy for whom he should do this:

For he loveth our nation, and he hath built us a synagogue.

Then Jesus went with them. And when he was now not far from the house, the centurion sent friends to him, saying unto him, Lord, trouble not thyself: for I am not worthy that thou shouldest enter under my roof:

Wherefore neither thought I myself worthy to come unto thee: but say in a word, and my servant shall be healed.

For I also am a man set under authority, having under me soldiers, and I say unto one, Go, and he goeth; and to another, Come, and he cometh; and to my servant, Do this, and he doeth it.

When Jesus heard these things, he marvelled at him, and turned him about, and said unto the people that followed him, I say unto you, I have not found so great faith, no, not in Israel.

And they that were sent, returning to the house, found the servant whole that had been sick.

—Luke 7:2–10

∞ And Recall the Power of Your Influence

Behold, I have taught you statutes and judgments, even as the LORD my God commanded me, that ye should do so in the land whither ye go to possess it.

Keep therefore and do them; for this is your wisdom and your understanding in the sight of the nations, which shall hear all these statutes, and say, Surely this great nation is a wise and understanding people.

—Deuteronomy 4:5–6

When I call to remembrance the unfeigned faith that is in thee, which dwelt first in thy grandmother Lois, and thy mother Eunice; and I am persuaded that in thee also.

—2 Timothy 1:5

Three

Watch Your Time!

Yes, you're busy. But keep making time for all the things that really matter—like family, the church, and the needs of the community. After all, as someone once said: "No one will ever come to the end of his life and regret spending too much time with the children."

Our God Cares about Time

The great thing, if one can, is to stop regarding all the unpleasant things as

41

*interruptions of one's "own," or "real" life.
The truth is of course that what one calls the
interruptions are precisely one's real life—
the life God is sending one day by day.*
—C. S. Lewis[1]

I have heard thee in a time accepted, and
in the day of salvation have I succoured
thee: behold, now is the accepted time;
behold, now is the day of salvation.

—*2 Corinthians 6:2*

But, beloved, be not ignorant of this one
thing, that one day is with the Lord as a
thousand years, and a thousand years as one
day.

—*2 Peter 3:8*

∞ *Struggling with Time Pressures?*

He giveth power to the faint; and to them
that have no might he increaseth strength.
Even the youths shall faint and be weary,
and the young men shall utterly fall:
But they that wait upon the Lord shall
renew their strength; they shall mount up

with wings as eagles; they shall run, and not
be weary; and they shall walk, and not faint.

—Isaiah 40:29–31

And the apostles gathered themselves
together unto Jesus, and told him all things,
both what they had done, and what they
had taught.

And he said unto them, Come ye yourselves
apart into a desert place, and rest a while: for
there were many coming and going, and they
had no leisure so much as to eat.

And they departed into a desert place by
ship privately.

—Mark 6:30–32

And he said unto me, My grace is
sufficient for thee: for my strength is made
perfect in weakness. Most gladly therefore
will I rather glory in my infirmities, that the
power of Christ may rest upon me.

Therefore I take pleasure in infirmities, in
reproaches, in necessities, in persecutions, in
distresses for Christ's sake: for when I am
weak, then am I strong.

—2 Corinthians 12:9–10

And let us not be weary in well doing: for in due season we shall reap, if we faint not.

—Galatians 6:9

∾ *Overwhelmed with Deadlines?*

The Egyptians pursued after them, all the horses and chariots of Pharaoh, and his horsemen, and his army, and overtook them encamping by the sea, beside Pi–hahiroth, before Baal–zephon.

And when Pharaoh drew nigh, the children of Israel lifted up their eyes, and, behold, the Egyptians marched after them; and they were sore afraid: and the children of Israel cried out unto the LORD.

—Exodus 14:9–10

Thou wilt keep him in perfect peace, whose mind is stayed on thee: because he trusteth in thee.

—Isaiah 26:3

For he shall be as a tree planted by the waters, and that spreadeth out her roots by the river, and shall not see when heat cometh, but her leaf shall be green; and shall not be careful in the year of drought, neither shall cease from yielding fruit.

—*Jeremiah 17:8*

Now it came to pass on a certain day, that he went into a ship with his disciples: and he said unto them, Let us go over unto the other side of the lake. And they launched forth.

But as they sailed he fell asleep: and there came down a storm of wind on the lake; and they were filled with water, and were in jeopardy.

And they came to him, and awoke him, saying, Master, master, we perish. Then he arose, and rebuked the wind and the raging of the water: and they ceased, and there was a calm.

And he said unto them, Where is your faith? And they being afraid wondered, saying one to another, What manner of man is this! for he commandeth even the winds and water, and they obey him.

—*Luke 8:22–25*

Peace I leave with you, my peace I give unto you: not as the world giveth, give I unto you. Let not your heart be troubled, neither let it be afraid.

—*John 14:27*

Be careful for nothing; but in every thing by prayer and supplication with thanksgiving let your requests be made known unto God.

And the peace of God, which passeth all understanding, shall keep your hearts and minds through Christ Jesus.

—*Philippians 4:6–7*

Stressed-Out with Projects?

Truly my soul waiteth upon God: from him cometh my salvation.

He only is my rock and my salvation; he is my defence; I shall not be greatly moved.

—*Psalm 62:1–2*

I waited patiently for the LORD; and he inclined unto me, and heard my cry.

He brought me up also out of an horrible pit, out of the miry clay, and set my feet upon a rock, and established my goings.

And he hath put a new song in my mouth, even praise unto our God: many shall see it, and fear, and shall trust in the LORD.

—Psalm 40:1–3

In the day of my trouble I sought the Lord: my sore ran in the night, and ceased not: my soul refused to be comforted.

I remembered God, and was troubled: I complained, and my spirit was overwhelmed.

Thou holdest mine eyes waking: I am so troubled that I cannot speak.

I have considered the days of old, the years of ancient times.

I call to remembrance my song in the night: I commune with mine own heart: and my spirit made diligent search.

—Psalm 77:2–6

≈ *Constantly Striving to Achieve?*

And he came to Capernaum: and being in the house he asked them, What was it that ye disputed among yourselves by the way?

But they held their peace: for by the way they had disputed among themselves, who should be the greatest.

And he sat down, and called the twelve, and saith unto them, If any man desire to be first, the same shall be last of all, and servant of all.

And he took a child, and set him in the midst of them: and when he had taken him in his arms, he said unto them,

Whosoever shall receive one of such children in my name, receiveth me: and whosoever shall receive me, receiveth not me, but him that sent me.

—*Mark 9:33–37*

And James and John, the sons of Zebedee, come unto him, saying, Master, we would that thou shouldest do for us whatsoever we shall desire.

And he said unto them, What would ye that I should do for you?

They said unto him, Grant unto us that we may sit, one on thy right hand, and the other on thy left hand, in thy glory.

But Jesus said unto them, Ye know not what ye ask: can ye drink of the cup that I drink of? and be baptized with the baptism that I am baptized with?

And they said unto him, We can. And Jesus said unto them, Ye shall indeed drink of the cup that I drink of; and with the baptism that I am baptized withal shall ye be baptized:

But to sit on my right hand and on my left hand is not mine to give; but it shall be given to them for whom it is prepared.

And when the ten heard it, they began to be much displeased with James and John.

But Jesus called them to him, and saith unto them, Ye know that they which are accounted to rule over the Gentiles exercise lordship over them; and their great ones exercise authority upon them.

But so shall it not be among you: but whosoever will be great among you, shall be your minister:

And whosoever of you will be the chiefest, shall be servant of all.

For even the Son of man came not to be ministered unto, but to minister, and to give his life a ransom for many.

—Mark 10:35–45

What profit hath a man of all his labour which he taketh under the sun?

One generation passeth away, and another generation cometh: but the earth abideth for ever.

The sun also ariseth, and the sun goeth down, and hasteth to his place where he arose.

The wind goeth toward the south, and turneth about unto the north; it whirleth about continually, and the wind returneth again according to his circuits.

All the rivers run into the sea; yet the sea is not full; unto the place from whence the rivers come, thither they return again.

All things are full of labour; man cannot utter it: the eye is not satisfied with seeing, nor the ear filled with hearing.

The thing that hath been, it is that which shall be; and that which is done is that which shall be done: and there is no new thing under the sun.

—Ecclesiastes 1:3–9

∽ *Letting Ambition Run Wild?*

And they said, Go to, let us build us a city and a tower, whose top may reach unto heaven; and let us make us a name, lest we be scattered abroad upon the face of the whole earth.

—Genesis 11:4

Make Good Use of the Time God Gives You

When God wanted sponges and oysters, He made them, and put one on a rock, and the other in the mud. When he made man,

He did not make him to be a sponge,
or an oyster; He made him with feet and
hands, and head, and heart,
and vital blood, and a place to use them,
and said to him. "Go, work!"

—*Henry Ward Beecher*[2]

Now it is high time to awake out of sleep:
for now is our salvation nearer than when
we believed.

—*Romans 13:11*

[Redeem] the time, because the days are
evil.

—*Ephesians 5:16*

Find Fulfillment in Doing God's Will

Many [people] have so much of their
identity invested in their jobs that when they
are forced to retire, they die—because they
see their life and value as inextricably
entwined with what they do. How tragic,

then, that so many men [and women] are trapped in stultifying jobs. Not even when they are at work can they find fulfillment.

—Christopher Harding[3]

Whoso trusteth in the LORD, happy is he.

—Proverbs 16:20

Acquaint now thyself with him, and be at peace: thereby good shall come unto thee.

Receive, I pray thee, the law from his mouth, and lay up his words in thine heart.

If thou return to the Almighty, thou shalt be built up, thou shalt put away iniquity far from thy tabernacles.

Then shalt thou lay up gold as dust, and the gold of Ophir as the stones of the brooks.

Yea, the Almighty shall be thy defence, and thou shalt have plenty of silver.

For then shalt thou have thy delight in the Almighty, and shalt lift up thy face unto God.

—Job 22:21–26

Happy art thou, O Israel: who is like unto thee, O people saved by the LORD, the shield of thy help, and who is the sword of thy excellency! And thine enemies shall be found liars unto thee; and thou shalt tread upon their high places.

—*Deuteronomy 33:29*

They shall be abundantly satisfied with the fatness of thy house; and thou shalt make them drink of the river of thy pleasures.

—*Psalm 36:8*

I delight to do thy will, O my God: yea, thy law is within my heart.

—*Psalm 40:8*

My soul shall be satisfied as with marrow and fatness; and my mouth shall praise thee with joyful lips.

—*Psalm 63:5*

Happy is he that hath the God of Jacob for his help, whose hope is in the LORD his God.

—*Psalm 146:5*

Remember: God Controls Your Future!

When all else is lost, the future still remains.
—*Christian Nestell Bovee*

Behold, I shew you a mystery; We shall not all sleep, but we shall all be changed,

In a moment, in the twinkling of an eye, at the last trump: for the trumpet shall sound, and the dead shall be raised incorruptible, and we shall be changed.

For this corruptible must put on incorruption, and this mortal must put on immortality.

So when this corruptible shall have put on incorruption, and this mortal shall have put on immortality, then shall be brought to pass the saying that is written, Death is swallowed up in victory.

O death, where is thy sting? O grave, where is thy victory?

The sting of death is sin; and the strength of sin is the law.

But thanks be to God, which giveth us the victory through our Lord Jesus Christ. Therefore, my beloved brethren, be ye stedfast, unmovable, always abounding in the work of the Lord, forasmuch as ye know that your labour is not in vain in the Lord.

—*1 Corinthians 15:51–58*

Four

Busy People Can Still Pray

"*I do my best praying in the car on the way to work*," said Renata. "*That's because it's about the only time I'm alone!*"

You know the story—people around you at work during the day and the family vying for your attention in the evening at home. When do you find the time to enter your "prayer closet"? Well, you also know that praying doesn't necessarily require folded hands and knees touching the floor. In fact, whenever you think of it, simply open your heart to the Lord. He's there, waiting to hear from you.

Learn to Pray!

I don't know of a single foreign product that enters this country untaxed, except the answer to prayer.

—Mark Twain

Before they call, I will answer; and while they are yet speaking, I will hear.

—*Isaiah 65:24*

And when thou prayest, thou shalt not be as the hypocrites are: for they love to pray standing in the synagogues and in the corners of the streets, that they may be seen of men. Verily I say unto you, They have their reward.

But thou, when thou prayest, enter into thy closet, and when thou hast shut thy door, pray to thy Father which is in secret; and thy Father which seeth in secret shall reward thee openly.

But when ye pray, use not vain repetitions, as the heathen do: for they think that they shall be heard for their much speaking.

Be not ye therefore like unto them: for your Father knoweth what things ye have need of, before ye ask him.

After this manner therefore pray ye: Our Father which art in heaven, Hallowed be thy name.

Thy kingdom come. Thy will be done in earth, as it is in heaven.

Give us this day our daily bread.

And forgive us our debts, as we forgive our debtors.

And lead us not into temptation, but deliver us from evil: For thine is the kingdom, and the power, and the glory, for ever. Amen.

—*Matthew 6:5–13*

And this is the confidence that we have in him, that, if we ask any thing according to his will, he heareth us:

And if we know that he hear us, whatsoever we ask, we know that we have the petitions that we desired of him.

—*1 John 5:14–15*

Ask, and it shall be given you; seek, and ye shall find; knock, and it shall be opened unto you:

For every one that asketh receiveth; and he that seeketh findeth; and to him that knocketh it shall be opened.

Or what man is there of you, whom if his son ask bread, will he give him a stone?

Or if he ask a fish, will he give him a serpent?

If ye then, being evil, know how to give good gifts unto your children, how much more shall your Father which is in heaven give good things to them that ask him?

—*Matthew 7:7–11*

Is any among you afflicted? let him pray. Is any merry? let him sing psalms.

Is any sick among you? let him call for the elders of the church; and let them pray over him, anointing him with oil in the name of the Lord:

And the prayer of faith shall save the sick, and the Lord shall raise him up; and if he hath committed sins, they shall be forgiven him.

Confess your faults one to another, and pray one for another, that ye may be healed. The effectual fervent prayer of a righteous man availeth much.

Elias was a man subject to like passions as we are, and he prayed earnestly that it might not rain: and it rained not on the earth by the space of three years and six months.

And he prayed again, and the heaven gave rain, and the earth brought forth her fruit.

—James 5:13–18

Let us draw near with a true heart in full assurance of faith, having our hearts sprinkled from an evil conscience, and our bodies washed with pure water.

—Hebrews 10:22

Let us therefore come boldly unto the throne of grace, that we may obtain mercy, and find grace to help in time of need.

—Hebrews 4:16

And whatsoever we ask, we receive of him, because we keep his commandments, and do those things that are pleasing in his sight.

—1 John 3:22

Emulate the Prayer Warriors of the Past

Pray as if everything depended on God, and work as if everything depended upon man.

—Francis Spellman

Pray without ceasing.

—1 Thessalonians 5:17

 Elijah

And call ye on the name of your gods, and I will call on the name of the LORD: and the God that answereth by fire, let him be God. And all the people answered and said, It is well spoken.

And Elijah said unto the prophets of Baal, Choose you one bullock for yourselves, and dress it first; for ye are many; and call on the name of your gods, but put no fire under.

And they took the bullock which was given them, and they dressed it, and called on the name of Baal from morning even until noon, saying, O Baal, hear us. But there was no voice, nor any that answered. And they leaped upon the altar which was made.

And it came to pass at noon, that Elijah mocked them, and said, Cry aloud: for he is a god; either he is talking, or he is pursuing, or he is in a journey, or peradventure he sleepeth, and must be awaked.

And they cried aloud, and cut themselves after their manner with knives and lancets, till the blood gushed out upon them.

And it came to pass, when midday was past, and they prophesied until the time of the offering of the evening sacrifice, that there was neither voice, nor any to answer, nor any that regarded.

And Elijah said unto all the people, Come near unto me. And all the people came near unto him. And he repaired the altar of the LORD that was broken down.

And Elijah took twelve stones, according to the number of the tribes of the sons of Jacob, unto whom the word of the LORD came, saying, Israel shall be thy name:

And with the stones he built an altar in the name of the LORD: and he made a trench about the altar, as great as would contain two measures of seed.

And he put the wood in order, and cut the bullock in pieces, and laid him on the wood, and said, Fill four barrels with water, and pour it on the burnt sacrifice, and on the wood.

And he said, Do it the second time. And they did it the second time. And he said, Do it the third time. And they did it the third time.

And the water ran round about the altar; and he filled the trench also with water.

And it came to pass at the time of the offering of the evening sacrifice, that Elijah the prophet came near, and said, LORD God of Abraham, Isaac, and of Israel, let it be known this day that thou art God in Israel, and that I am thy servant, and that I have done all these things at thy word.

Hear me, O LORD, hear me, that this people may know that thou art the LORD God, and that thou hast turned their heart back again.

Then the fire of the LORD fell, and consumed the burnt sacrifice, and the wood, and the stones, and the dust, and licked up the water that was in the trench.

And when all the people saw it, they fell on their faces: and they said, The LORD, he is the God; the LORD, he is the God.

—*1 Kings 18:24–39*

∾ *Abraham*

And Abraham drew near, and said, Wilt thou also destroy the righteous with the wicked?

Peradventure there be fifty righteous within the city: wilt thou also destroy and not spare the place for the fifty righteous that are therein?

That be far from thee to do after this manner, to slay the righteous with the wicked: and that the righteous should be as the wicked, that be far from thee: Shall not the Judge of all the earth do right?

And the LORD said, If I find in Sodom fifty righteous within the city, then I will spare all the place for their sakes.

And Abraham answered and said, Behold now, I have taken upon me to speak unto the Lord, which am but dust and ashes:

Peradventure there shall lack five of the fifty righteous: wilt thou destroy all the city for lack of five? And he said, If I find there forty and five, I will not destroy it.

And he spake unto him yet again, and said, Peradventure there shall be forty found there. And he said, I will not do it for forty's sake.

And he said unto him, Oh let not the Lord be angry, and I will speak: Peradventure there shall thirty be found there. And he said, I will not do it, if I find thirty there.

And he said, Behold now, I have taken upon me to speak unto the Lord:

Peradventure there shall be twenty found there. And he said, I will not destroy it for twenty's sake.

And he said, Oh let not the Lord be angry, and I will speak yet but this once: Peradventure ten shall be found there. And he said, I will not destroy it for ten's sake.

—Genesis 18:23–32

∾ *Moses*

And Moses cried unto the LORD, saying, Heal her now, O God, I beseech thee.

And the LORD said unto Moses, If her father had but spit in her face, should she not be ashamed seven days? let her be shut out from the camp seven days, and after that let her be received in again.

And Miriam was shut out from the camp seven days: and the people journeyed not till Miriam was brought in again.

—Numbers 12:13–15

∾ Gideon

And Gideon said unto God, If thou wilt save Israel by mine hand, as thou hast said,

Behold, I will put a fleece of wool in the floor; and if the dew be on the fleece only, and it be dry upon all the earth beside, then shall I know that thou wilt save Israel by mine hand, as thou hast said.

And it was so: for he rose up early on the morrow, and thrust the fleece together, and wringed the dew out of the fleece, a bowl full of water.

And Gideon said unto God, Let not thine anger be hot against me, and I will speak but this once: let me prove, I pray thee, but this once with the fleece; let it now be dry only upon the fleece, and upon all the ground let there be dew.

And God did so that night: for it was dry upon the fleece only, and there was dew on all the ground.

—Judges 6:36–40

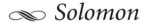

Jacob

And Jacob said, O God of my father Abraham, and God of my father Isaac, the LORD which saidst unto me, Return unto thy country, and to thy kindred, and I will deal well with thee:

I am not worthy of the least of all the mercies, and of all the truth, which thou hast shewed unto thy servant; for with my staff I passed over this Jordan; and now I am become two bands.

Deliver me, I pray thee, from the hand of my brother, from the hand of Esau: for I fear him, lest he will come and smite me, and the mother with the children.

And thou saidst, I will surely do thee good, and make thy seed as the sand of the sea, which cannot be numbered for multitude.

—Genesis 32:9–12

Solomon

And Solomon made affinity with Pharaoh king of Egypt, and took Pharaoh's daughter, and brought her into the city of David, until he had made an end of building his own house, and the house of the LORD, and the wall of Jerusalem round about.

Only the people sacrificed in high places, because there was no house built unto the name of the LORD, until those days.

And Solomon loved the LORD, walking in the statutes of David his father: only he sacrificed and burnt incense in high places.

And the king went to Gibeon to sacrifice there; for that was the great high place: a thousand burnt offerings did Solomon offer upon that altar.

In Gibeon the LORD appeared to Solomon in a dream by night: and God said, Ask what I shall give thee.

And Solomon said, Thou hast shewed unto thy servant David my father great mercy, according as he walked before thee in truth, and in righteousness, and in uprightness of heart with thee; and thou hast kept for him this great kindness, that thou hast given him a son to sit on his throne, as it is this day.

And now, O LORD my God, thou hast made thy servant king instead of David my father: and I am but a little child: I know not how to go out or come in.

And thy servant is in the midst of thy people which thou hast chosen, a great people, that cannot be numbered nor counted for multitude.

Give therefore thy servant an understanding heart to judge thy people, that I may discern between good and bad: for who is able to judge this thy so great a people?

And the speech pleased the Lord, that Solomon had asked this thing.

And God said unto him, Because thou hast asked this thing, and hast not asked for thyself long life; neither hast asked riches for thyself, nor hast asked the life of thine enemies; but hast asked for thyself understanding to discern judgment;

Behold, I have done according to thy words: lo, I have given thee a wise and an understanding heart; so that there was none like thee before thee, neither after thee shall any arise like unto thee.

And I have also given thee that which thou hast not asked, both riches, and honour: so that there shall not be any among the kings like unto thee all thy days.

—*1 Kings 3:1–13*

∞ *Hagar*

And the angel of the LORD found her by a fountain of water in the wilderness, by the fountain in the way to Shur.

And he said, Hagar, Sarai's maid, whence camest thou? and whither wilt thou go? And she said, I flee from the face of my mistress Sarai.

And the angel of the LORD said unto her, Return to thy mistress, and submit thyself under her hands.

And the angel of the LORD said unto her, I will multiply thy seed exceedingly, that it shall not be numbered for multitude.

And the angel of the LORD said unto her, Behold, thou art with child, and shalt bear a son, and shalt call his name Ishmael; because the LORD hath heard thy affliction.

And he will be a wild man; his hand will be against every man, and every man's hand against him; and he shall dwell in the presence of all his brethren.

And she called the name of the LORD that spake unto her, Thou God seest me: for she said, Have I also here looked after him that seeth me?

—*Genesis 16:7–13*

❧ *Samson*

And Samson called unto the LORD, and said, O Lord GOD, remember me, I pray thee, and strengthen me, I pray thee, only this once, O God, that I may be at once avenged of the Philistines for my two eyes.

And Samson took hold of the two middle pillars upon which the house stood, and on which it was borne up, of the one with his right hand, and of the other with his left.

And Samson said, Let me die with the Philistines. And he bowed himself with all his might; and the house fell upon the lords, and upon all the people that were therein.

So the dead which he slew at his death were more than they which he slew in his life.

—*Judges 16:28–30*

∾ *David*

And David enquired of the LORD, saying, Shall I go up to the Philistines? wilt thou deliver them into mine hand? And the LORD said unto David, Go up: for I will doubtless deliver the Philistines into thine hand.

And David came to Baal–perazim, and David smote them there, and said, The LORD hath broken forth upon mine enemies before me, as the breach of waters. Therefore he called the name of that place Baal–perazim.

And there they left their images, and David and his men burned them.

And the Philistines came up yet again, and spread themselves in the valley of Rephaim.

And when David enquired of the LORD, he said, Thou shalt not go up; but fetch a compass behind them, and come upon them over against the mulberry trees.

And let it be, when thou hearest the sound of a going in the tops of the mulberry trees, that then thou shalt bestir thyself: for then shall the LORD go out before thee, to smite the host of the Philistines.

And David did so, as the LORD had commanded him; and smote the Philistines from Geba until thou come to Gazer.

—*2 Samuel 5:19–25*

∾ *Hezekiah*

Thus shall ye speak to Hezekiah king of Judah, saying, Let not thy God in whom thou trustest deceive thee, saying, Jerusalem shall not be delivered into the hand of the king of Assyria.

Behold, thou hast heard what the kings of Assyria have done to all lands, by destroying them utterly: and shalt thou be delivered?

Have the gods of the nations delivered them which my fathers have destroyed; as Gozan, and Haran, and Rezeph, and the children of Eden which were in Thelasar?

Where is the king of Hamath, and the king of Arpad, and the king of the city of Sepharvaim, of Hena, and Ivah?

And Hezekiah received the letter of the hand of the messengers, and read it: and Hezekiah went up into the house of the LORD, and spread it before the LORD.

And Hezekiah prayed before the LORD, and said, O LORD God of Israel, which dwellest between the cherubims, thou art the God, even thou alone, of all the kingdoms of the earth; thou hast made heaven and earth.

LORD, bow down thine ear, and hear: open, LORD, thine eyes, and see: and hear the words of Sennacherib, which hath sent him to reproach the living God.

Of a truth, LORD, the kings of Assyria have destroyed the nations and their lands,

And have cast their gods into the fire: for they were no gods, but the work of men's hands, wood and stone: therefore they have destroyed them.

Now therefore, O LORD our God, I beseech thee, save thou us out of his hand, that all the kingdoms of the earth may know that thou art the LORD God, even thou only.

Then Isaiah the son of Amoz sent to Hezekiah, saying, Thus saith the LORD God of Israel, That which thou hast prayed to me against Sennacherib king of Assyria I have heard.

—*2 Kings 19:10–20*

In those days was Hezekiah sick unto death. And the prophet Isaiah the son of Amoz came to him, and said unto him, Thus saith the LORD, Set thine house in order; for thou shalt die, and not live.

Then he turned his face to the wall, and prayed unto the LORD, saying,

I beseech thee, O LORD, remember now how I have walked before thee in truth and with a perfect heart, and have done that which is good in thy sight. And Hezekiah wept sore.

And it came to pass, afore Isaiah was gone out into the middle court, that the word of the LORD came to him, saying,

Turn again, and tell Hezekiah the captain of my people, Thus saith the LORD, the God of David thy father, I have heard thy prayer, I have seen thy tears: behold, I will heal thee: on the third day thou shalt go up unto the house of the LORD.

And I will add unto thy days fifteen years; and I will deliver thee and this city out of the hand of the king of Assyria; and I will defend this city for mine own sake, and for my servant David's sake.

And Isaiah said, Take a lump of figs. And they took and laid it on the boil, and he recovered.

And Hezekiah said unto Isaiah, What shall be the sign that the LORD will heal me, and that I shall go up into the house of the LORD the third day?

And Isaiah said, This sign shalt thou have of the LORD, that the LORD will do the thing that he hath spoken: shall the shadow go forward ten degrees, or go back ten degrees?

And Hezekiah answered, It is a light thing for the shadow to go down ten degrees: nay, but let the shadow return backward ten degrees.

And Isaiah the prophet cried unto the LORD: and he brought the shadow ten

degrees backward, by which it had gone
down in the dial of Ahaz.

—2 Kings 20:1–11

∾ *Elijah*

And it came to pass at the time of the
offering of the evening sacrifice, that Elijah
the prophet came near, and said, LORD God
of Abraham, Isaac, and of Israel, let it be
known this day that thou art God in Israel,
and that I am thy servant, and that I have
done all these things at thy word.

Hear me, O LORD, hear me, that this
people may know that thou art the LORD
God, and that thou hast turned their heart
back again.

Then the fire of the LORD fell, and
consumed the burnt sacrifice, and the
wood, and the stones, and the dust, and
licked up the water that was in the trench.

—1 Kings 18:36–38

∾ *Elisha*

And Elisha prayed, and said, LORD, I pray thee, open his eyes, that he may see. And the LORD opened the eyes of the young man; and he saw: and, behold, the mountain was full of horses and chariots of fire round about Elisha.

And when they came down to him, Elisha prayed unto the LORD, and said, Smite this people, I pray thee, with blindness. And he smote them with blindness according to the word of Elisha.

And Elisha said unto them, This is not the way, neither is this the city: follow me, and I will bring you to the man whom ye seek. But he led them to Samaria.

And it came to pass, when they were come into Samaria, that Elisha said, LORD, open the eyes of these men, that they may see. And the LORD opened their eyes, and they saw; and, behold, they were in the midst of Samaria.

—2 Kings 6:17–20

∞ *Daniel*

Then was the secret revealed unto Daniel
in a night vision. Then Daniel blessed the
God of heaven.

Daniel answered and said, Blessed be the
name of God for ever and ever: for wisdom
and might are his:

And he changeth the times and the
seasons: he removeth kings, and setteth up
kings: he giveth wisdom unto the wise, and
knowledge to them that know
understanding:

He revealeth the deep and secret things:
he knoweth what is in the darkness, and the
light dwelleth with him.

I thank thee, and praise thee, O thou God
of my fathers, who hast given me wisdom
and might, and hast made known unto me
now what we desired of thee: for thou hast
now made known unto us the king's matter.

—Daniel 2:19–23

And whiles I was speaking, and praying,
and confessing my sin and the sin of my
people Israel, and presenting my

supplication before the LORD my God for the holy mountain of my God;

Yea, whiles I was speaking in prayer, even the man Gabriel, whom I had seen in the vision at the beginning, being caused to fly swiftly, touched me about the time of the evening oblation.

And he informed me, and talked with me, and said, O Daniel, I am now come forth to give thee skill and understanding.

At the beginning of thy supplications the commandment came forth, and I am come to shew thee; for thou art greatly beloved: therefore understand the matter, and consider the vision.

—*Daniel 9:20–23*

∾ *Jesus*

And he went a little further, and fell on his face, and prayed, saying, O my Father, if it be possible, let this cup pass from me: nevertheless not as I will, but as thou wilt.

And he cometh unto the disciples, and findeth them asleep, and saith unto Peter,

What, could ye not watch with me one hour?

Watch and pray, that ye enter not into temptation: the spirit indeed is willing, but the flesh is weak.

He went away again the second time, and prayed, saying, O my Father, if this cup may not pass away from me, except I drink it, thy will be done.

And he came and found them asleep again: for their eyes were heavy.

And he left them, and went away again, and prayed the third time, saying the same words.

—Matthew 26:39–44

∾ *Paul*

Wherefore I desire that ye faint not at my tribulations for you, which is your glory.

For this cause I bow my knees unto the Father of our Lord Jesus Christ,

Of whom the whole family in heaven and earth is named,

That he would grant you, according to the riches of his glory, to be strengthened with might by his Spirit in the inner man;

That Christ may dwell in your hearts by faith; that ye, being rooted and grounded in love,

May be able to comprehend with all saints what is the breadth, and length, and depth, and height;

And to know the love of Christ, which passeth knowledge, that ye might be filled with all the fulness of God.

Now unto him that is able to do exceeding abundantly above all that we ask or think, according to the power that worketh in us,

Unto him be glory in the church by Christ Jesus throughout all ages, world without end. Amen.

—*Ephesians 3:13–21*

Five

How's Your Witness on the Job?

We don't leave the Lord once we leave for the office. He's right there with us, all through the day. The question is: how willing are we to share Him with others? We can do it through our words, winsomely, at the appropriate moment. But most of the time, we'll portray our Christ through the actions and attitudes we display in our daily routine. So how will you respond to the next person who walks into your office?

Even at Work, Offer Good News!

The evangelistic harvest is always urgent. The destiny of men and of nations is always being decided. Every generation is strategic. We are not responsible for the past generation, and we cannot bear the full responsibility for the next one; but we do have our generation. God will hold us responsible as to how well we fulfill our responsibilities to this age and take advantage of our opportunities.

—*Billy Graham*

I say unto you, Whosoever shall confess me before men, him shall the Son of man also confess before the angels of God:

But he that denieth me before men shall be denied before the angels of God.

—*Luke 12:8–9*

Men, brethren, and fathers, hear ye my defence which I make now unto you.

(And when they heard that he spake in the Hebrew tongue to them, they kept the more silence: and he saith,)

I am verily a man which am a Jew, born in Tarsus, a city in Cilicia, yet brought up in this city at the feet of Gamaliel, and taught according to the perfect manner of the law of the fathers, and was zealous toward God, as ye all are this day.

And I persecuted this way unto the death, binding and delivering into prisons both men and women.

As also the high priest doth bear me witness, and all the estate of the elders: from whom also I received letters unto the brethren, and went to Damascus, to bring them which were there bound unto Jerusalem, for to be punished.

And it came to pass, that, as I made my journey, and was come nigh unto Damascus about noon, suddenly there shone from heaven a great light round about me.

And I fell unto the ground, and heard a voice saying unto me, Saul, Saul, why persecutest thou me?

And I answered, Who art thou, Lord? And he said unto me, I am Jesus of Nazareth, whom thou persecutest.

And they that were with me saw indeed the light, and were afraid; but they heard not the voice of him that spake to me.

And I said, What shall I do, Lord? And the Lord said unto me, Arise, and go into Damascus; and there it shall be told thee of all things which are appointed for thee to do.

And when I could not see for the glory of that light, being led by the hand of them that were with me, I came into Damascus.

And one Ananias, a devout man according to the law, having a good report of all the Jews which dwelt there,

Came unto me, and stood, and said unto me, Brother Saul, receive thy sight. And the same hour I looked up upon him.

And he said, The God of our fathers hath chosen thee, that thou shouldest know his will, and see that Just One, and shouldest hear the voice of his mouth.

For thou shalt be his witness unto all men of what thou hast seen and heard.

—Acts 22:1–15

Display Excellent Character Quailities at Work

Most of us can easily discern that falsifying tax records or pilfering supplies is wrong. But so many issues of integrity in the work place are gray areas, in which the line between right and wrong is blurred.

Is it altogether right, for example, to enthusiastically recommend someone for employment when you know of serious questions regarding that person's competence? Is it right to use your influence as a corporate executive to bump someone else off an over-booked flight and take his place yourself? . . . Questions like these are matters of conscience. That means that there are no explicit biblical instructions one way or the other, and there are no legal statutes involved.

—*Doug Sherman and William Hendricks*[1]

Whatsoever ye do, do it heartily, as to the Lord, and not unto men;

Knowing that of the Lord ye shall receive the reward of the inheritance: for ye serve the Lord Christ.

—Colossians 3:23–24

∞ *Live Out Biblical Principles*

Through wisdom is an house builded; and by understanding it is established.

—Proverbs 24:3

And wisdom and knowledge shall be the stability of thy times, and strength of salvation: the fear of the LORD is his treasure.

—Isaiah 33:6

Therefore whosoever heareth these sayings of mine, and doeth them, I will liken him unto a wise man, which built his house upon a rock:

And the rain descended, and the floods came, and the winds blew, and beat upon that house; and it fell not: for it was founded upon a rock.

And every one that heareth these sayings of mine, and doeth them not, shall be likened unto a foolish man, which built his house upon the sand:

And the rain descended, and the floods came, and the winds blew, and beat upon that house; and it fell: and great was the fall of it.

And it came to pass, when Jesus had ended these sayings, the people were astonished at his doctrine.

—*Matthew 7:24–28*

Yea, so have I strived to preach the gospel, not where Christ was named, lest I should build upon another man's foundation.

—*Romans 15:20*

For other foundation can no man lay than that is laid, which is Jesus Christ.

Now if any man build upon this foundation gold, silver, precious stones, wood, hay, stubble;

Every man's work shall be made manifest: for the day shall declare it, because it shall be revealed by fire; and the fire shall try every man's work of what sort it is.

If any man's work abide which he hath built thereupon, he shall receive a reward.

—*1 Corinthians 3:11–14*

∾ *Portray a Godly Lifestyle*

Ye are the light of the world. A city that is set on an hill cannot be hid.

Neither do men light a candle, and put it under a bushel, but on a candlestick; and it giveth light unto all that are in the house.

Let your light so shine before men, that they may see your good works, and glorify your Father which is in heaven.

—*Matthew 5:14–16*

If ye then be risen with Christ, seek those things which are above, where Christ sitteth on the right hand of God.

Set your affection on things above, not on things on the earth.

For ye are dead, and your life is hid with Christ in God.

When Christ, who is our life, shall appear, then shall ye also appear with him in glory.

Mortify therefore your members which are upon the earth; fornication, uncleanness, inordinate affection, evil concupiscence, and covetousness, which is idolatry:

For which things' sake the wrath of God cometh on the children of disobedience:

In the which ye also walked some time, when ye lived in them.

But now ye also put off all these; anger, wrath, malice, blasphemy, filthy communication out of your mouth.

Lie not one to another, seeing that ye have put off the old man with his deeds;

And have put on the new man, which is renewed in knowledge after the image of him that created him.

—*Colossians 3:1–10*

∽ Unite with Other Believers at Work

Endeavouring to keep the unity of the Spirit in the bond of peace.

—Ephesians 4:3

Till we all come in the unity of the faith, and of the knowledge of the Son of God, unto a perfect man, unto the measure of the stature of the fulness of Christ.

—Ephesians 4:13

As touching brotherly love ye need not that I write unto you: for ye yourselves are taught of God to love one another.

And indeed ye do it toward all the brethren which are in all Macedonia: but we beseech you, brethren, that ye increase more and more;

And that ye study to be quiet, and to do your own business, and to work with your own hands, as we commanded you;

That ye may walk honestly toward them that are without, and that ye may have lack of nothing.

—1 Thessalonians 4:9–12

∾ *Display Initiative*

And beside this, giving all diligence, add to your faith virtue; and to virtue knowledge;

And to knowledge temperance; and to temperance patience; and to patience godliness;

And to godliness brotherly kindness; and to brotherly kindness charity.

For if these things be in you, and abound, they make you that ye shall neither be barren nor unfruitful in the knowledge of our Lord Jesus Christ.

But he that lacketh these things is blind, and cannot see afar off, and hath forgotten that he was purged from his old sins.

—*2 Peter 1:5–9*

Be Ready with Wise Responses

The great spiritual task facing me is to so fully trust that I belong to God that I can be free in the world—free to speak even when my words are not received; free to act even when my actions are criticized, ridiculed, or considered useless; free also to receive love from people and to be grateful for all the signs of God's presence in the world. I am convinced that I will truly be able to love the world when I fully believe that I am loved far beyond its boundaries.

—*Henri Nouwen*[2]

Walk in wisdom toward them that are without, redeeming the time.

Let your speech be always with grace, seasoned with salt, that ye may know how ye ought to answer every man.

—*Colossians 4:5–6*

If Necessary, Risk All for Christ

Fight the temptation to be bashful about the Christian faith. Avoid a bashful brand of Christian that tiptoes up to people and

*hesitating suggests: "I may be wrong, but I'm
afraid that if you do not repent after a
fashion and receive Christ, so to speak, you
might be damned, as it were."*

—William A. Ward

Hereunto were ye called: because Christ
also suffered for us, leaving us an example,
that ye should follow his steps.

—1 Peter 2:21

And Jesus stood before the governor: and
the governor asked him, saying, Art thou
the King of the Jews? And Jesus said unto
him, Thou sayest.

And when he was accused of the chief
priests and elders, he answered nothing.

Then said Pilate unto him, Hearest thou
not how many things they witness against
thee?

And he answered him to never a word;
insomuch that the governor marvelled
greatly.

Now at that feast the governor was wont
to release unto the people a prisoner, whom
they would.

And they had then a notable prisoner, called Barabbas.

Therefore when they were gathered together, Pilate said unto them, Whom will ye that I release unto you? Barabbas, or Jesus which is called Christ?

For he knew that for envy they had delivered him.

When he was set down on the judgment seat, his wife sent unto him, saying, Have thou nothing to do with that just man: for I have suffered many things this day in a dream because of him.

But the chief priests and elders persuaded the multitude that they should ask Barabbas, and destroy Jesus.

The governor answered and said unto them, Whether of the twain will ye that I release unto you? They said, Barabbas.

Pilate saith unto them, What shall I do then with Jesus which is called Christ? They all say unto him, Let him be crucified.

And the governor said, Why, what evil hath he done? But they cried out the more, saying, Let him be crucified.

—*Matthew 27:11–23*

And Stephen, full of faith and power, did great wonders and miracles among the people.

Then there arose certain of the synagogue, which is called the synagogue of the Libertines, and Cyrenians, and Alexandrians, and of them of Cilicia and of Asia, disputing with Stephen.

And they were not able to resist the wisdom and the spirit by which he spake.

Then they suborned men, which said, We have heard him speak blasphemous words against Moses, and against God.

And they stirred up the people, and the elders, and the scribes, and came upon him, and caught him, and brought him to the council,

And set up false witnesses, which said, This man ceaseth not to speak blasphemous words against this holy place, and the law:

For we have heard him say, that this Jesus of Nazareth shall destroy this place, and shall change the customs which Moses delivered us.

And all that sat in the council, looking stedfastly on him, saw his face as it had been the face of an angel.

—*Acts 6:8–15*

Six

Leadership: Make These Folks Your Mentors

*T*he Bible abounds with stories of great leaders. Most of these men and women knew exactly how to take charge and gather a following. They inspired and encouraged. They led by example while demonstrating the quality of a true servant's heart. And they could do it because they, themselves, were following the Master of the Universe.

Who Are You Following?

Virtuous men do good by setting themselves up as models before the public. But I do good by setting myself up as a warning.
—*Michel de Montaigne*

[Thou] art confident that thou thyself art a guide of the blind, a light of them which are in darkness,

An instructor of the foolish, a teacher of babes, which hast the form of knowledge and of the truth in the law.

Thou therefore which teachest another, teachest thou not thyself? thou that preachest a man should not steal, dost thou steal?

Thou that sayest a man should not commit adultery, dost thou commit adultery? thou that abhorrest idols, dost thou commit sacrilege?

Thou that makest thy boast of the law, through breaking the law dishonourest thou God?

For the name of God is blasphemed among the Gentiles through you, as it is written.

For circumcision verily profiteth, if thou keep the law: but if thou be a breaker of the law, thy circumcision is made uncircumcision.

—*Romans 2:19–25*

Beloved, believe not every spirit, but try the spirits whether they are of God: because many false prophets are gone out into the world.

Hereby know ye the Spirit of God: Every spirit that confesseth that Jesus Christ is come in the flesh is of God:

And every spirit that confesseth not that Jesus Christ is come in the flesh is not of God: and this is that spirit of antichrist, whereof ye have heard that it should come; and even now already is it in the world.

Ye are of God, little children, and have overcome them: because greater is he that is in you, than he that is in the world.

They are of the world: therefore speak they of the world, and the world heareth them.

—*1 John 4:1–5*

For many deceivers are entered into the world, who confess not that Jesus Christ is come in the flesh. This is a deceiver and an antichrist.

Look to yourselves, that we lose not those things which we have wrought, but that we receive a full reward.

Whosoever transgresseth, and abideth not in the doctrine of Christ, hath not God. He that abideth in the doctrine of Christ, he hath both the Father and the Son.

If there come any unto you, and bring not this doctrine, receive him not into your house, neither bid him God speed.

—*2 John 7–10*

How Well Are You Leading?

Take heed to yourselves also because there are many eyes upon you.
So there will be many who observe your fall.
If you miscarry, the world will also echo with it. It is the same as the eclipses

of the sun in broad daylight—
they are seldom without witnesses.

—*Richard Baxter*[1]

∾ Deborah: Demonstrating Mentoring

And Deborah, a prophetess, the wife of Lapidoth, she judged Israel at that time.

And she dwelt under the palm tree of Deborah between Ramah and Bethel in mount Ephraim: and the children of Israel came up to her for judgment.

And she sent and called Barak the son of Abinoam out of Kedesh-naphtali, and said unto him, Hath not the LORD God of Israel commanded, saying, Go and draw toward mount Tabor, and take with thee ten thousand men of the children of Naphtali and of the children of Zebulun?

And I will draw unto thee to the river Kishon Sisera, the captain of Jabin's army, with his chariots and his multitude; and I will deliver him into thine hand.

And Barak said unto her, If thou wilt go with me, then I will go: but if thou wilt not go with me, then I will not go.

And she said, I will surely go with thee: notwithstanding the journey that thou takest shall not be for thine honour; for the LORD shall sell Sisera into the hand of a woman. And Deborah arose, and went with Barak to Kedesh.

—Judges 4:4–9

Then sang Deborah and Barak the son of Abinoam on that day, saying,

Praise ye the LORD for the avenging of Israel, when the people willingly offered themselves.

Hear, O ye kings; give ear, O ye princes; I, even I, will sing unto the LORD; I will sing praise to the LORD God of Israel.

LORD, when thou wentest out of Seir, when thou marchedst out of the field of Edom, the earth trembled, and the heavens dropped, the clouds also dropped water.

The mountains melted from before the LORD, even that Sinai from before the LORD God of Israel.

In the days of Shamgar the son of Anath, in the days of Jael, the highways were unoccupied, and the travellers walked through byways.

The inhabitants of the villages ceased, they ceased in Israel, until that I Deborah arose, that I arose a mother in Israel.

They chose new gods; then was war in the gates: was there a shield or spear seen among forty thousand in Israel?

My heart is toward the governors of Israel, that offered themselves willingly among the people. Bless ye the LORD.

Speak, ye that ride on white asses, ye that sit in judgment, and walk by the way.

They that are delivered from the noise of archers in the places of drawing water, there shall they rehearse the righteous acts of the LORD, even the righteous acts toward the inhabitants of his villages in Israel: then shall the people of the LORD go down to the gates.

Awake, awake, Deborah: awake, awake, utter a song: arise, Barak, and lead thy captivity captive, thou son of Abinoam.

—*Judges 5:1–12*

∞ Moses: Leading in Spite of Personal Limitations

And Moses said unto God, Who am I, that I should go unto Pharaoh, and that I should bring forth the children of Israel out of Egypt? . . .

O my Lord, I am not eloquent, neither heretofore, nor since thou hast spoken unto thy servant: but I am slow of speech, and of a slow tongue.

—*Exodus 3:11; 4:10*

And [God] said, Certainly I will be with thee; and this shall be a token unto thee, that I have sent thee: When thou hast brought forth the people out of Egypt, ye shall serve God upon this mountain.

And Moses said unto God, Behold, when I come unto the children of Israel, and shall say unto them, The God of your fathers hath sent me unto you; and they shall say to me, What is his name? what shall I say unto them?

And God said unto Moses, I AM THAT I AM: and he said, Thus shalt thou say unto the children of Israel, I AM hath sent me unto you.

And God said moreover unto Moses, Thus shalt thou say unto the children of Israel, The LORD God of your fathers, the God of Abraham, the God of Isaac, and the God of Jacob, hath sent me unto you: this is my name for ever, and this is my memorial unto all generations.

Go, and gather the elders of Israel together, and say unto them, The LORD God of your fathers, the God of Abraham, of Isaac, and of Jacob, appeared unto me, saying, I have surely visited you, and seen that which is done to you in Egypt:

And I have said, I will bring you up out of the affliction of Egypt unto the land of the Canaanites, and the Hittites, and the Amorites, and the Perizzites, and the Hivites, and the Jebusites, unto a land flowing with milk and honey.

And they shall hearken to thy voice: and thou shalt come, thou and the elders of Israel, unto the king of Egypt, and ye shall say unto him, The LORD God of the Hebrews hath met with us: and now let us go, we beseech thee, three days' journey into the wilderness, that we may sacrifice to the LORD our God.

And I am sure that the king of Egypt will not let you go, no, not by a mighty hand.

And I will stretch out my hand, and smite Egypt with all my wonders which I will do in the midst thereof: and after that he will let you go.

And I will give this people favour in the sight of the Egyptians: and it shall come to pass, that, when ye go, ye shall not go empty.

—*Exodus 3:12–21*

∞ *Caleb and Joshua: Leading Courageously Amidst Opposition*

Joshua the son of Nun, and Caleb the son of Jephunneh, which were of them that searched the land, rent their clothes:

And they spake unto all the company of the children of Israel, saying, The land, which we passed through to search it, is an exceeding good land.

If the LORD delight in us, then he will bring us into this land, and give it us; a land which floweth with milk and honey.

Only rebel not ye against the LORD, neither fear ye the people of the land; for they are bread for us: their defence is departed from them, and the LORD is with us: fear them not.

But all the congregation bade stone them with stones. And the glory of the LORD appeared in the tabernacle of the congregation before all the children of Israel.

—*Numbers 14:6–10*

Doubtless ye shall not come into the land, concerning which I sware to make you dwell therein, save Caleb the son of Jephunneh, and Joshua the son of Nun. . . .

But Joshua the son of Nun, and Caleb the son of Jephunneh, which were of the men that went to search the land, lived still.

—*Numbers 14:30, 38*

For they have wholly followed the LORD.

—*Numbers 32:12*

∽ *Gideon: Overcoming Low Self-Esteem*

Oh my Lord, wherewith shall I save Israel? behold, my family is poor in Manasseh, and I am the least in my father's house.

—*Judges 6:15*

And the LORD said unto him, Surely I will be with thee, and thou shalt smite the Midianites as one man. . . .

Then the angel of the LORD put forth the end of the staff that was in his hand, and touched the flesh and the unleavened cakes; and there rose up fire out of the rock, and consumed the flesh and the unleavened cakes. Then the angel of the LORD departed out of his sight.

And when Gideon perceived that he was an angel of the LORD, Gideon said, Alas, O Lord GOD! for because I have seen an angel of the LORD face to face.

And the LORD said unto him, Peace be unto thee; fear not: thou shalt not die.

Then Gideon built an altar there unto the LORD, and called it Jehovah-shalom: unto this day it is yet in Ophrah of the Abi-ezrites.

—*Judges 6:16, 21–24*

∾ *Esther: Leading with a Spirit of Self-Sacrifice*

Again Esther spake unto Hatach, and gave him commandment unto Mordecai;

All the king's servants, and the people of the king's provinces, do know, that whosoever, whether man or woman, shall come unto the king into the inner court, who is not called, there is one law of his to put him to death, except such to whom the king shall hold out the golden sceptre, that he may live: but I have not been called to come in unto the king these thirty days.

And they told to Mordecai Esther's words.

Then Mordecai commanded to answer Esther, Think not with thyself that thou shalt escape in the king's house, more than all the Jews.

For if thou altogether holdest thy peace at this time, then shall there enlargement and deliverance arise to the Jews from another place; but thou and thy father's house shall be destroyed: and who knoweth whether thou art come to the kingdom for such a time as this?

Then Esther bade them return Mordecai this answer,

Go, gather together all the Jews that are present in Shushan, and fast ye for me, and neither eat nor drink three days, night or day: I also and my maidens will fast likewise; and so will I go in unto the king, which is not according to the law: and if I perish, I perish.

So Mordecai went his way, and did according to all that Esther had commanded him.

—*Esther 4:10–17*

 ## Lois and Eunice: Raising a Great Pastor

I thank God, whom I serve from my forefathers with pure conscience, that without ceasing I have remembrance of thee in my prayers night and day;

Greatly desiring to see thee, being mindful of thy tears, that I may be filled with joy;

When I call to remembrance the unfeigned faith that is in thee, which dwelt first in thy grandmother Lois, and thy mother Eunice; and I am persuaded that in thee also.

Wherefore I put thee in remembrance that thou stir up the gift of God, which is in thee by the putting on of my hands.

—*2 Timothy 1:3–6*

⧓ *Mary: Responding Well to New Information*

And in the sixth month the angel Gabriel was sent from God unto a city of Galilee, named Nazareth,

To a virgin espoused to a man whose name was Joseph, of the house of David; and the virgin's name was Mary.

And the angel came in unto her, and said, Hail, thou that art highly favoured, the Lord is with thee: blessed art thou among women.

And when she saw him, she was troubled at his saying, and cast in her mind what manner of salutation this should be.

And the angel said unto her, Fear not, Mary: for thou hast found favour with God.

And, behold, thou shalt conceive in thy womb, and bring forth a son, and shalt call his name JESUS. . . .

And Mary said, My soul doth magnify the Lord,

And my spirit hath rejoiced in God my Saviour.

For he hath regarded the low estate of his handmaiden: for, behold, from henceforth all generations shall call me blessed.

For he that is mighty hath done to me great things; and holy is his name.

And his mercy is on them that fear him from generation to generation.

He hath shewed strength with his arm; he hath scattered the proud in the imagination of their hearts.

He hath put down the mighty from their seats, and exalted them of low degree.

He hath filled the hungry with good things; and the rich he hath sent empty away.

—*Luke 1:26–31, 46–53*

✷ *Joseph: Being Able to Forgive*

Then Joseph could not refrain himself before all them that stood by him; and he cried, Cause every man to go out from me. And there stood no man with him, while Joseph made himself known unto his brethren.

And he wept aloud: and the Egyptians and the house of Pharaoh heard.

And Joseph said unto his brethren, I am Joseph; doth my father yet live? And his brethren could not answer him; for they were troubled at his presence.

And Joseph said unto his brethren, Come near to me, I pray you. And they came near. And he said, I am Joseph your brother, whom ye sold into Egypt.

Now therefore be not grieved, nor angry
with yourselves, that ye sold me hither: for
God did send me before you to preserve life.

—*Genesis 45:1–5*

∾ *David: Being Able to Admit a Mistake*

And the LORD sent Nathan unto David.
And he came unto him, and said unto him,
There were two men in one city; the one
rich, and the other poor.

The rich man had exceeding many flocks
and herds:

But the poor man had nothing, save one
little ewe lamb, which he had bought and
nourished up: and it grew up together with
him, and with his children; it did eat of his
own meat, and drank of his own cup, and
lay in his bosom, and was unto him as a
daughter.

And there came a traveller unto the rich
man, and he spared to take of his own flock
and of his own herd, to dress for the
wayfaring man that was come unto him;
but took the poor man's lamb, and dressed

it for the man that was come to him.

And David's anger was greatly kindled against the man; and he said to Nathan, As the LORD liveth, the man that hath done this thing shall surely die:

And he shall restore the lamb fourfold, because he did this thing, and because he had no pity.

And Nathan said to David, Thou art the man. Thus saith the LORD God of Israel, I anointed thee king over Israel, and I delivered thee out of the hand of Saul;

And I gave thee thy master's house, and thy master's wives into thy bosom, and gave thee the house of Israel and of Judah; and if that had been too little, I would moreover have given unto thee such and such things.

Wherefore hast thou despised the commandment of the LORD, to do evil in his sight? thou hast killed Uriah the Hittite with the sword, and hast taken his wife to be thy wife, and hast slain him with the sword of the children of Ammon.

Now therefore the sword shall never depart from thine house; because thou hast despised me, and hast taken the wife of Uriah the Hittite to be thy wife.

Thus saith the LORD, Behold, I will raise up evil against thee out of thine own house, and I will take thy wives before thine eyes, and give them unto thy neighbour, and he shall lie with thy wives in the sight of this sun.

For thou didst it secretly: but I will do this thing before all Israel, and before the sun.

And David said unto Nathan, I have sinned against the LORD.

—2 Samuel 12:1–13

✺ *Timothy: Continuing to Learn*

Let no man despise thy youth; but be thou an example of the believers, in word, in conversation, in charity, in spirit, in faith, in purity.

—1 Timothy 4:12

Paul, an apostle of Jesus Christ by the will of God, according to the promise of life which is in Christ Jesus,

To Timothy, my dearly beloved son: Grace, mercy, and peace, from God the Father and Christ Jesus our Lord.

I thank God, whom I serve from my forefathers with pure conscience, that without ceasing I have remembrance of thee in my prayers night and day;

Greatly desiring to see thee, being mindful of thy tears, that I may be filled with joy;

When I call to remembrance the unfeigned faith that is in thee, which dwelt first in thy grandmother Lois, and thy mother Eunice; and I am persuaded that in thee also.

Wherefore I put thee in remembrance that thou stir up the gift of God, which is in thee by the putting on of my hands.

For God hath not given us the spirit of fear; but of power, and of love, and of a sound mind.

—2 Timothy 1:1–7

Thou therefore, my son, be strong in the grace that is in Christ Jesus.

And the things that thou hast heard of me among many witnesses, the same commit thou to faithful men, who shall be able to teach others also.

Thou therefore endure hardness, as a good soldier of Jesus Christ.

No man that warreth entangleth himself with the affairs of this life; that he may please him who hath chosen him to be a soldier.

And if a man also strive for masteries, yet is he not crowned, except he strive lawfully.

The husbandman that laboureth must be first partaker of the fruits.

Consider what I say; and the Lord give thee understanding in all things.

Remember that Jesus Christ of the seed of David was raised from the dead according to my gospel:

Wherein I suffer trouble, as an evildoer, even unto bonds; but the word of God is not bound.

Therefore I endure all things for the elect's sakes, that they may also obtain the salvation which is in Christ Jesus with eternal glory.

It is a faithful saying: For if we be dead with him, we shall also live with him:

If we suffer, we shall also reign with him: if we deny him, he also will deny us:

If we believe not, yet he abideth faithful: he cannot deny himself.

—*2 Timothy 2:1–13*

But thou hast fully known my doctrine, manner of life, purpose, faith, longsuffering, charity, patience,

Persecutions, afflictions, which came unto me at Antioch, at Iconium, at Lystra; what persecutions I endured: but out of them all the Lord delivered me.

—*2 Timothy 3:10–11*

Seven

Good Leaders Make Good Decisions

"I don't really enjoy making tough decisions, but it's pretty much my job description," says Mike. "Anyway, when it comes to business decisions, I know I can gather the facts and project the pros and cons pretty accurately. It's harder making decisions about my life's direction for the future. In those cases it's more a matter of listening for the Spirit's still, small

voice of guidance—and looking to biblical principles. I know that at those times, I have to be 'still' myself. And maybe that's the hardest part of all."

God Cares about Our Decisions

Is there any greater wretchedness than to taste the dregs of our own insufficiency and misery and hopelessness . . . ? Yet it is blessed to be reduced to these depths if, in them, we can find God. Until we have reached the bottom of the abyss, there is still something for us to choose between all and nothing. There is still something in between. We can still evade the decision. When we are reduced to our last extreme, there is no further evasion. The choice is a terrible one . . . when we who have been destroyed and seem to be in hell miraculously choose God!

—*Thomas Merton*[1]

I have set before you life and death,
blessing and cursing: therefore choose life,
that both thou and thy seed may live.

—*Deuteronomy 30:19*

Abide in me, and I in you. As the branch
cannot bear fruit of itself, except it abide in the
vine; no more can ye, except ye abide in me.

I am the vine, ye are the branches: He
that abideth in me, and I in him, the same
bringeth forth much fruit: for without me
ye can do nothing.

If a man abide not in me, he is cast forth
as a branch, and is withered; and men
gather them, and cast them into the fire,
and they are burned.

If ye abide in me, and my words abide in
you, ye shall ask what ye will, and it shall be
done unto you.

Herein is my Father glorified, that ye bear
much fruit; so shall ye be my disciples.

As the Father hath loved me, so have I
loved you: continue ye in my love.

—*John 15:4–9*

Beware Indecision!

We have a choice: to plow new ground or let the weeds grow.

—*Jonathan Westover*

Elijah came unto all the people, and said, How long halt ye between two opinions? if the LORD be God, follow him: but if Baal, then follow him. And the people answered him not a word.

—*1 Kings 18:21*

Their heart is divided; now shall they be found faulty: he shall break down their altars, he shall spoil their images.

—*Hosea 10:2*

No man can serve two masters: for either he will hate the one, and love the other; or else he will hold to the one, and despise the other. Ye cannot serve God and mammon.

—*Matthew 6:24*

Watch and pray, that ye enter not into temptation: the spirit indeed is willing, but the flesh is weak.

—Matthew 26:41

A double minded man is unstable in all his ways.

—James 1:8

Go to now, ye that say, Today or tomorrow we will go into such a city, and continue there a year, and buy and sell, and get gain:

Whereas ye know not what shall be on the morrow. For what is your life? It is even a vapour, that appeareth for a little time, and then vanisheth away.

For that ye ought to say, If the Lord will, we shall live, and do this, or that.

But now ye rejoice in your boastings: all such rejoicing is evil.

Therefore to him that knoweth to do good, and doeth it not, to him it is sin.

—James 4:13–17

Avoid Second-Guessing

I hate to see things done by halves.
If it be right, do it boldly,—
if it be wrong leave it undone.

—*Bernard Gilpin*

∾ *The Israelites at the Red Sea*

And it was told the king of Egypt that the people fled: and the heart of Pharaoh and of his servants was turned against the people, and they said, Why have we done this, that we have let Israel go from serving us?

And he made ready his chariot, and took his people with him:

And he took six hundred chosen chariots, and all the chariots of Egypt, and captains over every one of them.

And the LORD hardened the heart of Pharaoh king of Egypt, and he pursued after the children of Israel: and the children of Israel went out with an high hand.

But the Egyptians pursued after them, all the horses and chariots of Pharaoh, and his horsemen, and his army, and overtook them encamping by the sea, beside Pi–hahiroth, before Baal–zephon.

And when Pharaoh drew nigh, the children of Israel lifted up their eyes, and, behold, the Egyptians marched after them; and they were sore afraid: and the children of Israel cried out unto the LORD.

And they said unto Moses, Because there were no graves in Egypt, hast thou taken us away to die in the wilderness? wherefore hast thou dealt thus with us, to carry us forth out of Egypt?

Is not this the word that we did tell thee in Egypt, saying, Let us alone, that we may serve the Egyptians? For it had been better for us to serve the Egyptians, than that we should die in the wilderness.

—*Exodus 14:5–12*

∾ Reluctant Warriors at Ai

And Joshua sent men from Jericho to Ai, which is beside Beth–aven, on the east side of Beth–el, and spake unto them, saying, Go up and view the country. And the men went up and viewed Ai.

And they returned to Joshua, and said unto him, Let not all the people go up; but let about two or three thousand men go up and smite Ai; and make not all the people to labour thither; for they are but few.

So there went up thither of the people about three thousand men: and they fled before the men of Ai.

And the men of Ai smote of them about thirty and six men: for they chased them from before the gate even unto Shebarim, and smote them in the going down: wherefore the hearts of the people melted, and became as water.

And Joshua rent his clothes, and fell to the earth upon his face before the ark of the LORD until the eventide, he and the elders of Israel, and put dust upon their heads.

And Joshua said, Alas, O Lord GOD, wherefore hast thou at all brought this people over Jordan, to deliver us into the hand of the Amorites, to destroy us? would to God we had been content, and dwelt on the other side Jordan!

O Lord, what shall I say, when Israel turneth their backs before their enemies!

For the Canaanites and all the inhabitants of the land shall hear of it, and shall environ us round, and cut off our name from the earth: and what wilt thou do unto thy great name?

And the LORD said unto Joshua, Get thee up; wherefore liest thou thus upon thy face?

—*Joshua 7:2–10*

∾ *Some Fickle Leaders*

The people answered him, We have heard out of the law that Christ abideth for ever: and how sayest thou, The Son of man must be lifted up? who is this Son of man?

Then Jesus said unto them, Yet a little while is the light with you. Walk while ye have the light, lest darkness come upon you: for he that walketh in darkness knoweth not whither he goeth.

While ye have light, believe in the light, that ye may be the children of light. These things spake Jesus, and departed, and did hide himself from them.

But though he had done so many miracles before them, yet they believed not on him:

That the saying of Esaias the prophet might be fulfilled, which he spake, Lord, who hath believed our report? and to whom hath the arm of the Lord been revealed?

Therefore they could not believe, because that Esaias said again,

He hath blinded their eyes, and hardened their heart; that they should not see with their eyes, nor understand with their heart, and be converted, and I should heal them.

These things said Esaias, when he saw his glory, and spake of him.

Nevertheless among the chief rulers also many believed on him; but because of the Pharisees they did not confess him, lest they should be put out of the synagogue:

For they loved the praise of men more than the praise of God.

—*John 12:34–43*

⚭ Felix Postponing a Decision

And herein do I exercise myself, to have always a conscience void of offense toward God, and toward men.

Now after many years I came to bring alms to my nation, and offerings.

Whereupon certain Jews from Asia found me purified in the temple, neither with multitude, nor with tumult.

Who ought to have been here before thee, and object, if they had ought against me.

Or else let these same here say, if they have found any evil doing in me, while I stood before the council,

Except it be for this one voice, that I cried standing among them, Touching the resurrection of the dead I am called in question by you this day.

And when Felix heard these things, having more perfect knowledge of that way, he deferred them, and said, When Lysias the chief captain shall come down, I will know the uttermost of your matter.

And he commanded a centurion to keep Paul, and to let him have liberty, and that he should forbid none of his acquaintance to minister or come unto him.

And after certain days, when Felix came with his wife Drusilla, which was a Jewess, he sent for Paul, and heard him concerning the faith in Christ.

And as he reasoned of righteousness, temperance, and judgment to come, Felix trembled, and answered, Go thy way for this time; when I have a convenient season, I will call for thee.

He hoped also that money should have been given him of Paul, that he might loose him: wherefore he sent for him the oftener, and communed with him.

But after two years Porcius Festus came into Felix' room: and Felix, willing to shew the Jews a pleasure, left Paul bound.

—*Acts 24:16–27*

Instead, Decide—and Stick With It!

When possible make the decisions now, even if action is in the future.

*A reviewed decision usually is better
than one reached at the last moment.*

— *William B. Given, Jr.*

Hold fast the form of sound words,
which thou hast heard of me, in faith and
love which is in Christ Jesus.

That good thing which was committed
unto thee keep by the Holy Ghost which
dwelleth in us.

—*2 Timothy 1:13–14*

Be sober, be vigilant; because your
adversary the devil, as a roaring lion, walketh
about, seeking whom he may devour:

Whom resist stedfast in the faith, knowing
that the same afflictions are accomplished in
your brethren that are in the world.

—*1 Peter 5:8–9*

That which ye have already hold fast till I
come.

And he that overcometh, and keepeth my
works unto the end, to him will I give
power over the nations.

—*Revelation 2:25–26*

These Folks Made Excellent Choices . . .

The block of granite which was an obstacle in the pathway of the weak becomes a stepping-stone in the pathway of the strong.

—Thomas Carlyle

∾ *Joseph*

And it came to pass after these things, that his master's wife cast her eyes upon Joseph; and she said, Lie with me.

But he refused, and said unto his master's wife, Behold, my master wotteth not what is with me in the house, and he hath committed all that he hath to my hand;

There is none greater in this house than I; neither hath he kept back any thing from me but thee, because thou art his wife: how then can I do this great wickedness, and sin against God?

And it came to pass, as she spake to Joseph day by day, that he hearkened not unto her, to lie by her, or to be with her.

And it came to pass about this time, that Joseph went into the house to do his business; and there was none of the men of the house there within.

And she caught him by his garment, saying, Lie with me: and he left his garment in her hand, and fled, and got him out.

And it came to pass, when she saw that he had left his garment in her hand, and was fled forth,

That she called unto the men of her house, and spake unto them, saying, See, he hath brought in an Hebrew unto us to mock us; he came in unto me to lie with me, and I cried with a loud voice:

And it came to pass, when he heard that I lifted up my voice and cried, that he left his garment with me, and fled, and got him out.

And she laid up his garment by her, until his lord came home.

And she spake unto him according to these words, saying, The Hebrew servant, which thou hast brought unto us, came in unto me to mock me:

And it came to pass, as I lifted up my voice and cried, that he left his garment with me, and fled out.

And it came to pass, when his master heard the words of his wife, which she spake unto him, saying, After this manner did thy servant to me; that his wrath was kindled.

And Joseph's master took him, and put him into the prison, a place where the king's prisoners were bound: and he was there in the prison.

—Genesis 39:7–20

∽ *Moses*

By faith Moses, when he was come to years, refused to be called the son of Pharaoh's daughter;

Choosing rather to suffer affliction with the people of God, than to enjoy the pleasures of sin for a season;

Esteeming the reproach of Christ greater riches than the treasures in Egypt: for he had respect unto the recompence of the reward.

—Hebrews 11:24–26

∞ *Balaam*

And Balak sent yet again princes, more, and more honourable than they.

And they came to Balaam, and said to him, Thus saith Balak the son of Zippor, Let nothing, I pray thee, hinder thee from coming unto me:

For I will promote thee unto very great honour, and I will do whatsoever thou sayest unto me: come therefore, I pray thee, curse me this people.

And Balaam answered and said unto the servants of Balak, If Balak would give me his house full of silver and gold, I cannot go beyond the word of the LORD my God, to do less or more.

—Numbers 22:15–18

∞ *Phinehas*

And when Phinehas, the son of Eleazar, the son of Aaron the priest, saw it, he rose up from among the congregation, and took a javelin in his hand;

And he went after the man of Israel into the tent, and thrust both of them through, the man of Israel, and the woman through her belly. So the plague was stayed from the children of Israel.

And those that died in the plague were twenty and four thousand.

And the LORD spake unto Moses, saying,

Phinehas, the son of Eleazar, the son of Aaron the priest, hath turned my wrath away from the children of Israel, while he was zealous for my sake among them, that I consumed not the children of Israel in my jealousy.

Wherefore say, Behold, I give unto him my covenant of peace:

And he shall have it, and his seed after him, even the covenant of an everlasting priesthood; because he was zealous for his God, and made an atonement for the children of Israel.

—Numbers 25:7–13

✎ *Abigail*

But one of the young men told Abigail, Nabal's wife, saying, Behold, David sent messengers out of the wilderness to salute our master; and he railed on them.

But the men were very good unto us, and we were not hurt, neither missed we any thing, as long as we were conversant with them, when we were in the fields:

They were a wall unto us both by night and day, all the while we were with them keeping the sheep.

Now therefore know and consider what thou wilt do; for evil is determined against our master, and against all his household: for he is such a son of Belial, that a man cannot speak to him.

Then Abigail made haste, and took two hundred loaves, and two bottles of wine, and five sheep ready dressed, and five measures of parched corn, and an hundred clusters of raisins, and two hundred cakes of figs, and laid them on asses.

And she said unto her servants, Go on before me; behold, I come after you. But she told not her husband Nabal.

And it was so, as she rode on the ass, that she came down by the covert of the hill, and, behold, David and his men came down against her; and she met them.

Now David had said, Surely in vain have I kept all that this fellow hath in the wilderness, so that nothing was missed of all that pertained unto him: and he hath requited me evil for good.

So and more also do God unto the enemies of David, if I leave of all that pertain to him by the morning light any that pisseth against the wall.

And when Abigail saw David, she hasted, and lighted off the ass, and fell before David on her face, and bowed herself to the ground,

And fell at his feet, and said, Upon me, my lord, upon me let this iniquity be: and let thine handmaid, I pray thee, speak in thine audience, and hear the words of thine handmaid.

Let not my lord, I pray thee, regard this man of Belial, even Nabal: for as his name is, so is he; Nabal is his name, and folly is with him: but I thine handmaid saw not the young men of my lord, whom thou didst send.

Now therefore, my lord, as the LORD liveth, and as thy soul liveth, seeing the LORD hath withholden thee from coming to shed blood, and from avenging thyself with thine own hand, now let thine enemies, and they that seek evil to my lord, be as Nabal.

And now this blessing which thine handmaid hath brought unto my lord, let it even be given unto the young men that follow my lord.

I pray thee, forgive the trespass of thine handmaid: for the LORD will certainly make my lord a sure house; because my lord fighteth the battles of the LORD, and evil hath not been found in thee all thy days.

Yet a man is risen to pursue thee, and to seek thy soul: but the soul of my lord shall be bound in the bundle of life with the LORD thy God; and the souls of thine enemies, them shall he sling out, as out of the middle of a sling.

And it shall come to pass, when the LORD shall have done to my lord according to all the good that he hath spoken concerning thee, and shall have appointed thee ruler over Israel;

That this shall be no grief unto thee, nor offence of heart unto my lord, either that thou hast shed blood causeless, or that my lord hath avenged himself: but when the LORD shall have dealt well with my lord, then remember thine handmaid.

And David said to Abigail, Blessed be the LORD God of Israel, which sent thee this day to meet me.

—1 Samuel 25:14–32

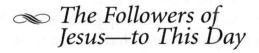 *The Followers of Jesus—to This Day*

Then Peter said, Lo, we have left all, and followed thee.

—Luke 18:28

145

Then Simon Peter answered him, Lord, to whom shall we go? thou hast the words of eternal life.

And we believe and are sure that thou art that Christ, the Son of the living God.

—John 6:68–69

According to my earnest expectation and my hope, that in nothing I shall be ashamed, but that with all boldness, as always, so now also Christ shall be magnified in my body, whether it be by life, or by death.

For to me to live is Christ, and to die is gain.

—Philippians 1:20–21

I have fought a good fight, I have finished my course, I have kept the faith:

Henceforth there is laid up for me a crown of righteousness, which the Lord, the righteous judge, shall give me at that day: and not to me only, but unto all them also that love his appearing.

—2 Timothy 4:7–8

Eight

Rely on the Lord as You Pursue the Bottom Line

Look at all you've accomplished so far. And you're hoping to gather more good things into the storehouse, right?

There's no problem in pursuing success with dogged determination. But in your quiet moments, deep in your heart of hearts, realize the truth of your life: everything you are and everything you have—all of it—comes directly from God's gracious hand.

It's true, isn't it? It's all a gift.

God Blesses Hard Work

Why would a loving God put His children to work as soon as He created them? Because He knew human labor was a blessing. He knew it would provide them challenges, excitement, adventure, and rewards that nothing else would. He knew that creatures made in His image needed to devote their time to meaningful tasks.

—Bill Hybels[1]

He that tilleth his land shall be satisfied with bread: but he that followeth vain persons is void of understanding. . . .

The hand of the diligent shall bear rule: but the slothful shall be under tribute.

Heaviness in the heart of man maketh it stoop: but a good word maketh it glad.

The righteous is more excellent than his neighbour: but the way of the wicked seduceth them.

The slothful man roasteth not that which he took in hunting: but the substance of a diligent man is precious.

—*Proverbs 12:11, 24–27*

Be thou diligent to know the state of thy flocks, and look well to thy herds.

For riches are not for ever: and doth the crown endure to every generation?

The hay appeareth, and the tender grass sheweth itself, and herbs of the mountains are gathered.

The lambs are for thy clothing, and the goats are the price of the field.

And thou shalt have goats' milk enough for thy food, for the food of thy household, and for the maintenance for thy maidens.

—*Proverbs 27:23–27*

The ants are a people not strong, yet they prepare their meat in the summer;

The conies are but a feeble folk, yet make they their houses in the rocks;

The locusts have no king, yet go they forth all of them by bands;

The spider taketh hold with her hands,
and is in kings' palaces.

—Proverbs 30:25–28

She seeketh wool, and flax, and worketh
willingly with her hands.

She is like the merchants' ships; she
bringeth her food from afar.

She riseth also while it is yet night, and
giveth meat to her household, and a portion
to her maidens.

She considereth a field, and buyeth it:
with the fruit of her hands she planteth a
vineyard.

She girdeth her loins with strength, and
strengtheneth her arms.

She perceiveth that her merchandise is
good: her candle goeth not out by night.

She layeth her hands to the spindle, and
her hands hold the distaff.

She stretcheth out her hand to the poor;
yea, she reacheth forth her hands to the
needy.

She is not afraid of the snow for her
household: for all her household are clothed
with scarlet.

She maketh herself coverings of tapestry; her clothing is silk and purple.

Her husband is known in the gates, when he sitteth among the elders of the land.

She maketh fine linen, and selleth it; and delivereth girdles unto the merchant.

Strength and honour are her clothing; and she shall rejoice in time to come.

She openeth her mouth with wisdom; and in her tongue is the law of kindness.

She looketh well to the ways of her household, and eateth not the bread of idleness.

—Proverbs 31:13–27

I have coveted no man's silver, or gold, or apparel.

Yea, ye yourselves know, that these hands have ministered unto my necessities, and to them that were with me.

—Acts 20:33–34

Know ye not that they which run in a race run all, but one receiveth the prize? So run, that ye may obtain.

And every man that striveth for the mastery is temperate in all things. Now they do it to obtain a corruptible crown; but we an incorruptible.

I therefore so run, not as uncertainly; so fight I, not as one that beateth the air:

But I keep under my body, and bring it into subjection: lest that by any means, when I have preached to others, I myself should be a castaway.

—1 Corinthians 9:24–27

And that ye study to be quiet, and to do your own business, and to work with your own hands, as we commanded you;

That ye may walk honestly toward them that are without, and that ye may have lack of nothing.

—1 Thessalonians 4:11–12

For even when we were with you, this we commanded you, that if any would not work, neither should he eat.

For we hear that there are some which walk among you disorderly, working not at all, but are busybodies.

Now them that are such we command
and exhort by our Lord Jesus Christ, that
with quietness they work, and eat their own
bread.

—*2 Thessalonians 3:10–12*

Concerned about Potential Failure?

*It's an old adage that the way to be safe is
never to be secure. . . . Each one of us
requires the spur of insecurity to force us to
do our best.*

—*Harold W. Dodds*

Commit thy works unto the LORD, and
thy thoughts shall be established.

—*Proverbs 16:3*

The LORD is nigh unto them that are of a
broken heart; and saveth such as be of a
contrite spirit.

—*Psalm 34:18*

We have this treasure in earthen vessels, that the excellency of the power may be of God, and not of us.

We are troubled on every side, yet not distressed; we are perplexed, but not in despair;

Persecuted, but not forsaken; cast down, but not destroyed;

Always bearing about in the body the dying of the Lord Jesus, that the life also of Jesus might be made manifest in our body.

For we which live are alway delivered unto death for Jesus' sake, that the life also of Jesus might be made manifest in our mortal flesh.

—2 Corinthians 4:7–11

Six days thou shalt do thy work, and on the seventh day thou shalt rest: that thine ox and thine ass may rest, and the son of thy handmaid, and the stranger, may be refreshed.

—Exodus 23:12

Thou wilt keep him in perfect peace, whose mind is stayed on thee: because he trusteth in thee.

—Isaiah 26:3

Consecrate All Your Dealings to the Lord . . .

Take my life and let it be

Consecrated, Lord, to Thee . . .

Take my hands, and let them move

At the impulse of Thy love.

—*Frances Ridley Havergal*

And she vowed a vow, and said, O LORD of hosts, if thou wilt indeed look on the affliction of thine handmaid, and remember me, and not forget thine handmaid, but wilt give unto thine handmaid a man child, then I will give him unto the LORD all the days of his life, and there shall no razor come upon his head. . . .

And when she had weaned him, she took him up with her, with three bullocks, and one ephah of flour, and a bottle of wine, and brought him unto the house of the LORD in Shiloh: and the child was young.

And they slew a bullock, and brought the child to Eli.

And she said, Oh my lord, as thy soul liveth, my lord, I am the woman that stood by thee here, praying unto the LORD.

For this child I prayed; and the LORD hath given me my petition which I asked of him:

Therefore also I have lent him to the LORD; as long as he liveth he shall be lent to the LORD. And he worshipped the LORD there.

—*1 Samuel 1:11, 24–28*

The sacrifices of God are a broken spirit: a broken and a contrite heart, O God, thou wilt not despise.

—*Psalm 51:17*

And Abel, he also brought of the firstlings of his flock and of the fat thereof. And the LORD had respect unto Abel and to his offering:

But unto Cain and to his offering he had not respect. And Cain was very wroth, and his countenance fell.

And the LORD said unto Cain, Why art thou wroth? and why is thy countenance fallen?

If thou doest well, shalt thou not be accepted? and if thou doest not well, sin lieth at the door.

—*Genesis 4:4–7*

And this they did, not as we hoped, but first gave their own selves to the Lord, and unto us by the will of God.

—*2 Corinthians 8:5*

. . . And Don't Worry about Money!

Riches are the pettiest and least worthy gifts which God can give a man. What are they to God's Word, to bodily gifts, such as beauty and health; or to the gifts of the mind, such as understanding, skill, wisdom?
Yet men toil for them day and night, and take not rest. Therefore God commonly gives riches to foolish people to whom he gives nothing else.

—*Martin Luther*

Therefore I say unto you, Take no thought for your life, what ye shall eat, or what ye shall drink; nor yet for your body, what ye shall put on. Is not the life more than meat, and the body than raiment?

Behold the fowls of the air: for they sow not, neither do they reap, nor gather into barns; yet your heavenly Father feedeth them. Are ye not much better than they?

Which of you by taking thought can add one cubit unto his stature?

And why take ye thought for raiment? Consider the lilies of the field, how they grow; they toil not, neither do they spin:

And yet I say unto you, That even Solomon in all his glory was not arrayed like one of these.

Wherefore, if God so clothe the grass of the field, which to day is, and to morrow is cast into the oven, shall he not much more clothe you, O ye of little faith?

Therefore take no thought, saying, What shall we eat? or, What shall we drink? or, Wherewithal shall we be clothed?

(For after all these things do the Gentiles seek:) for your heavenly Father knoweth that ye have need of all these things.

But seek ye first the kingdom of God, and his righteousness; and all these things shall be added unto you.

Take therefore no thought for the morrow: for the morrow shall take thought for the things of itself. Sufficient unto the day is the evil thereof.

—Matthew 6:25–34

Be careful for nothing; but in every thing by prayer and supplication with thanksgiving let your requests be made known unto God.

And the peace of God, which passeth all understanding, shall keep your hearts and minds through Christ Jesus. . . .

Not that I speak in respect of want: for I have learned, in whatsoever state I am, therewith to be content.

I know both how to be abased, and I know how to abound: every where and in all things I am instructed both to be full and to be hungry, both to abound and to suffer need.

I can do all things through Christ which strengtheneth me.

—Philippians 4:6–7, 11–13

∾ *Practice Good Stewardship*

The earth is the LORD'S, and the fulness thereof; the world, and they that dwell therein.

For he hath founded it upon the seas, and established it upon the floods.

—Psalm 24:1–2

What? know ye not that your body is the temple of the Holy Ghost which is in you, which ye have of God, and ye are not your own?

For ye are bought with a price: therefore glorify God in your body, and in your spirit, which are God's.

—1 Corinthians 6:19–20

And Jesus entered and passed through Jericho.

And, behold, there was a man named Zacchaeus, which was the chief among the publicans, and he was rich.

And he sought to see Jesus who he was; and could not for the press, because he was little of stature.

And he ran before, and climbed up into a sycomore tree to see him: for he was to pass that way.

And when Jesus came to the place, he looked up, and saw him, and said unto him, Zacchaeus, make haste, and come down; for to day I must abide at thy house.

And he made haste, and came down, and received him joyfully.

And when they saw it, they all murmured, saying, That he was gone to be guest with a man that is a sinner.

And Zacchaeus stood, and said unto the Lord; Behold, Lord, the half of my goods I give to the poor; and if I have taken any thing from any man by false accusation, I restore him fourfold.

And Jesus said unto him, This day is salvation come to this house, forsomuch as he also is a son of Abraham.

For the Son of man is come to seek and to save that which was lost.

—*Luke 19:1–10*

And when James, Cephas, and John, who seemed to be pillars, perceived the grace that was given unto me, they gave to me and Barnabas the right hands of fellowship; that we should go unto the heathen, and they unto the circumcision.

Only they would that we should remember the poor; the same which I also was forward to do.

—*Galatians 2:9–10*

But thou, O man of God, flee these things; and follow after righteousness, godliness, faith, love, patience, meekness.

Fight the good fight of faith, lay hold on eternal life, whereunto thou art also called, and hast professed a good profession before many witnesses.

I give thee charge in the sight of God, who quickeneth all things, and before Christ Jesus, who before Pontius Pilate witnessed a good confession;

That thou keep this commandment without spot, unrebukeable, until the appearing of our Lord Jesus Christ:

Which in his times he shall shew, who is the blessed and only Potentate, the King of kings, and Lord of lords;

Who only hath immortality, dwelling in the light which no man can approach unto; whom no man hath seen, nor can see: to whom be honour and power everlasting. Amen.

Charge them that are rich in this world, that they be not highminded, nor trust in uncertain riches, but in the living God, who giveth us richly all things to enjoy;

That they do good, that they be rich in good works, ready to distribute, willing to communicate;

Laying up in store for themselves a good foundation against the time to come, that they may lay hold on eternal life.

—*1 Timothy 6:11–19*

As every man hath received the gift, even so minister the same one to another, as good stewards of the manifold grace of God.

If any man speak, let him speak as the oracles of God; if any man minister, let him do it as of the ability which God giveth: that God in all things may be glorified through Jesus Christ, to whom be praise and dominion for ever and ever. Amen.

—*1 Peter 4:10–11*

∞ *Use Possessions Wisely and Frugally*

And he gathered up all the food of the seven years, which were in the land of Egypt, and laid up the food in the cities: the food of the field, which was round about every city, laid he up in the same.

And Joseph gathered corn as the sand of the sea, very much, until he left numbering; for it was without number.

And unto Joseph were born two sons before the years of famine came, which

Asenath the daughter of Poti–pherah priest of On bare unto him.

And Joseph called the name of the firstborn Manasseh: For God, said he, hath made me forget all my toil, and all my father's house.

And the name of the second called he Ephraim: For God hath caused me to be fruitful in the land of my affliction.

And the seven years of plenteousness, that was in the land of Egypt, were ended.

And the seven years of dearth began to come, according as Joseph had said: and the dearth was in all lands; but in all the land of Egypt there was bread.

—*Genesis 41:48–54*

And the children of Israel did so, and gathered, some more, some less.

And when they did mete it with an omer, he that gathered much had nothing over, and he that gathered little had no lack; they gathered every man according to his eating.

And Moses said, Let no man leave of it till the morning.

Notwithstanding they hearkened not unto Moses; but some of them left of it until the morning, and it bred worms, and stank: and Moses was wroth with them.

And they gathered it every morning, every man according to his eating: and when the sun waxed hot, it melted.

And it came to pass, that on the sixth day they gathered twice as much bread, two omers for one man: and all the rulers of the congregation came and told Moses.

And he said unto them, This is that which the LORD hath said, To morrow is the rest of the holy sabbath unto the LORD: bake that which ye will bake to day, and seethe that ye will seethe; and that which remaineth over lay up for you to be kept until the morning.

And they laid it up till the morning, as Moses bade: and it did not stink, neither was there any worm therein.

—*Exodus 16:17–24*

So he went and did according unto the word of the LORD: for he went and dwelt by the brook Cherith, that is before Jordan.

And the ravens brought him bread and flesh in the morning, and bread and flesh in the evening; and he drank of the brook.

And it came to pass after a while, that the brook dried up, because there had been no rain in the land.

And the word of the LORD came unto him, saying,

Arise, get thee to Zarephath, which belongeth to Zidon, and dwell there: behold, I have commanded a widow woman there to sustain thee.

So he arose and went to Zarephath. And when he came to the gate of the city, behold, the widow woman was there gathering of sticks: and he called to her, and said, Fetch me, I pray thee, a little water in a vessel, that I may drink.

And as she was going to fetch it, he called to her, and said, Bring me, I pray thee, a morsel of bread in thine hand.

And she said, As the LORD thy God liveth, I have not a cake, but an handful of meal in a barrel, and a little oil in a cruse: and, behold, I am gathering two sticks, that I may go in and dress it for me and my son, that we may eat it, and die.

And Elijah said unto her, Fear not; go and do as thou hast said: but make me thereof a little cake first, and bring it unto me, and after make for thee and for thy son.

—*1 Kings 17:5–13*

A good man leaveth an inheritance to his children's children: and the wealth of the sinner is laid up for the just.

—*Proverbs 13:22*

He that loveth pleasure shall be a poor man: he that loveth wine and oil shall not be rich.

The wicked shall be a ransom for the righteous, and the transgressor for the upright.

It is better to dwell in the wilderness, than with a contentious and an angry woman.

There is treasure to be desired and oil in the dwelling of the wise; but a foolish man spendeth it up.

He that followeth after righteousness and mercy findeth life, righteousness, and honour.

—*Proverbs 21:17–21*

Be not among winebibbers; among riotous eaters of flesh:

For the drunkard and the glutton shall come to poverty: and drowsiness shall clothe a man with rags.

—*Proverbs 23:20–21*

And they did all eat, and were filled: and they took up of the broken meat that was left seven baskets full.

—*Matthew 15:37*

And when James, Cephas, and John, who seemed to be pillars, perceived the grace that was given unto me, they gave to me and Barnabas the right hands of fellowship; that we should go unto the heathen, and they unto the circumcision.

Only they would that we should remember the poor; the same which I also was forward to do.

—*Galatians 2:9–10*

$\mathscr{P}$arables for $\mathscr{P}$rofessionals

In your business life, you have to teach every day. And you know it's important to do it effectively. The biblical writers knew it, too; and they often used stories to make their points, just as Jesus did.

Are you ready to learn from these great biblical stories? Much that comes through can be applied directly to business. So soak in the teachings of God's Word!

Old Testament Parables: Ancient Wisdom for All

Scripture tells us that we must become like little children, and that the teaching we need is right here if we have eyes to see and ears to hear. It tells us that we live and move and have our being in a divine One who is already at home in us, ready to guide us where we need to go. It tells us that Holy Wisdom cries in the streets for us, promising that in self-abandonment we will never be abandoned. It assures us that we will find what we seek, that we shall know the truth, and that it will make us free.

—Gerald May[1]

Wisdom crieth without; she uttereth her voice in the streets:

She crieth in the chief place of concourse, in the openings of the gates: in the city she uttereth her words, saying,

How long, ye simple ones, will ye love simplicity?

—*Proverbs 1:20–22*

∾ *Choose Leadership Wisely*

The trees went forth on a time to anoint a king over them; and they said unto the olive tree, Reign thou over us.

But the olive tree said unto them, Should I leave my fatness, wherewith by me they honour God and man, and go to be promoted over the trees?

And the trees said to the fig tree, Come thou, and reign over us.

But the fig tree said unto them, Should I forsake my sweetness, and my good fruit, and go to be promoted over the trees?

Then said the trees unto the vine, Come thou, and reign over us.

And the vine said unto them, Should I leave my wine, which cheereth God and man, and go to be promoted over the trees?

Then said all the trees unto the bramble, Come thou, and reign over us.

And the bramble said unto the trees, If in truth ye anoint me king over you, then come and put your trust in my shadow: and if not, let fire come out of the bramble, and devour the cedars of Lebanon.

—*Judges 9:8–15*

∽ Be Prepared to Change Course

And the LORD sent Nathan unto David. And he came unto him, and said unto him, There were two men in one city; the one rich, and the other poor.

The rich man had exceeding many flocks and herds:

But the poor man had nothing, save one little ewe lamb, which he had bought and nourished up: and it grew up together with him, and with his children; it did eat of his own meat, and drank of his own cup, and lay in his bosom, and was unto him as a daughter.

And there came a traveller unto the rich man, and he spared to take of his own flock and of his own herd, to dress for the

wayfaring man that was come unto him;
but took the poor man's lamb, and dressed
it for the man that was come to him.

And David's anger was greatly kindled
against the man; and he said to Nathan, As
the LORD liveth, the man that hath done this
thing shall surely die:

And he shall restore the lamb fourfold,
because he did this thing, and because he
had no pity.

—2 Samuel 12:1–6

∞ *Pay Attention to Maintenance Needs*

Thou hast brought a vine out of Egypt:
thou hast cast out the heathen, and planted
it.

Thou preparedst room before it, and
didst cause it to take deep root, and it filled
the land.

The hills were covered with the shadow of
it, and the boughs thereof were like the
goodly cedars.

She sent out her boughs unto the sea, and
her branches unto the river.

Why hast thou then broken down her hedges, so that all they which pass by the way do pluck her?

The boar out of the wood doth waste it, and the wild beast of the field doth devour it.

Return, we beseech thee, O God of hosts: look down from heaven, and behold, and visit this vine;

And the vineyard which thy right hand hath planted, and the branch that thou madest strong for thyself.

It is burned with fire, it is cut down: they perish at the rebuke of thy countenance.

—*Psalm 80:8–16*

Now will I sing to my well-beloved a song of my beloved touching his vineyard. My well-beloved hath a vineyard in a very fruitful hill:

And he fenced it, and gathered out the stones thereof, and planted it with the choicest vine, and built a tower in the midst of it, and also made a winepress therein: and he looked that it should bring forth grapes, and it brought forth wild grapes.

And now, O inhabitants of Jerusalem, and men of Judah, judge, I pray you, betwixt me and my vineyard.

What could have been done more to my vineyard, that I have not done in it? wherefore, when I looked that it should bring forth grapes, brought it forth wild grapes?

And now go to; I will tell you what I will do to my vineyard: I will take away the hedge thereof, and it shall be eaten up; and break down the wall thereof, and it shall be trodden down:

And I will lay it waste: it shall not be pruned, nor digged; but there shall come up briers and thorns: I will also command the clouds that they rain no rain upon it.

For the vineyard of the LORD of hosts is the house of Israel, and the men of Judah his pleasant plant: and he looked for judgment, but behold oppression; for righteousness, but behold a cry.

—*Isaiah 5:1–7*

Give ye ear, and hear my voice; hearken, and hear my speech.

Doth the plowman plow all day to sow? doth he open and break the clods of his ground?

When he hath made plain the face thereof, doth he not cast abroad the fitches, and scatter the cummin, and cast in the principal wheat and the appointed barley and the rie in their place?

For his God doth instruct him to discretion, and doth teach him.

For the fitches are not threshed with a threshing instrument, neither is a cart wheel turned about upon the cummin; but the fitches are beaten out with a staff, and the cummin with a rod.

Bread corn is bruised; because he will not ever be threshing it, nor break it with the wheel of his cart, nor bruise it with his horsemen.

This also cometh forth from the LORD of hosts, which is wonderful in counsel, and excellent in working.

—*Isaiah 28:23–29*

Parables in the New Testament: Excellent Relational Principles

You cannot teach a [person] anything; you can only help him find it within himself.

—Galileo

∞ No Discrimination!

And he became very hungry, and would have eaten: but while they made ready, he fell into a trance,

And saw heaven opened, and a certain vessel descending unto him, as it had been a great sheet knit at the four corners, and let down to the earth:

Wherein were all manner of fourfooted beasts of the earth, and wild beasts, and creeping things, and fowls of the air.

And there came a voice to him, Rise, Peter; kill, and eat.

But Peter said, Not so, Lord; for I have never eaten any thing that is common or unclean.

And the voice spake unto him again the second time, What God hath cleansed, that call not thou common.

This was done thrice: and the vessel was received up again into heaven.

—*Acts 10:10–16*

❧ *Remember Your Roots*

For it is written, that Abraham had two sons, the one by a bondmaid, the other by a freewoman.

But he who was of the bondwoman was born after the flesh; but he of the freewoman was by promise.

Which things are an allegory: for these are the two covenants; the one from the mount Sinai, which gendereth to bondage, which is Agar.

For this Agar is mount Sinai in Arabia, and answereth to Jerusalem which now is, and is in bondage with her children.

But Jerusalem which is above is free, which is the mother of us all.

For it is written, Rejoice, thou barren that bearest not; break forth and cry, thou that travailest not: for the desolate hath many more children than she which hath an husband.

Now we, brethren, as Isaac was, are the children of promise.

But as then he that was born after the flesh persecuted him that was born after the Spirit, even so it is now.

Nevertheless what saith the scripture? Cast out the bondwoman and her son: for the son of the bondwoman shall not be heir with the son of the freewoman.

So then, brethren, we are not children of the bondwoman, but of the free.

—*Galatians 4:22–31*

∞ *Stay Ethically Pure*

But in a great house there are not only vessels of gold and of silver, but also of wood and of earth; and some to honour, and some to dishonour.

If a man therefore purge himself from these, he shall be a vessel unto honour, sanctified, and meet for the master's use, and prepared unto every good work.

—*2 Timothy 2:20–21*

∽ *Do What You Say*

For if any be a hearer of the word, and not a doer, he is like unto a man beholding his natural face in a glass:

For he beholdeth himself, and goeth his way, and straightway forgetteth what manner of man he was.

But whoso looketh into the perfect law of liberty, and continueth therein, he being not a forgetful hearer, but a doer of the work, this man shall be blessed in his deed.

—*James 1:23–25*

Parables of Jesus: They Apply to Business!

I am always ready to learn, but I do not always like being taught.

—*Winston Churchill*

That it might be fulfilled which was spoken by the prophet, saying, I will open

181

my mouth in parables; I will utter things which have been kept secret from the foundation of the world.

—*Matthew 13:35*

∞ *Build on a Solid Foundation*

Whosoever cometh to me, and heareth my sayings, and doeth them, I will shew you to whom he is like:

He is like a man which built an house, and digged deep, and laid the foundation on a rock: and when the flood arose, the stream beat vehemently upon that house, and could not shake it: for it was founded upon a rock.

But he that heareth, and doeth not, is like a man that without a foundation built an house upon the earth; against which the stream did beat vehemently, and immediately it fell; and the ruin of that house was great.

—*Luke 6:47–49*

∞ Treat Debtors with Compassion

There was a certain creditor which had two debtors: the one owed five hundred pence, and the other fifty.

And when they had nothing to pay, he frankly forgave them both. Tell me therefore, which of them will love him most?

Simon answered and said, I suppose that he, to whom he forgave most. And he said unto him, Thou hast rightly judged.

And he turned to the woman, and said unto Simon, Seest thou this woman? I entered into thine house, thou gavest me no water for my feet: but she hath washed my feet with tears, and wiped them with the hairs of her head.

Thou gavest me no kiss: but this woman since the time I came in hath not ceased to kiss my feet.

My head with oil thou didst not anoint: but this woman hath anointed my feet with ointment.

Wherefore I say unto thee, Her sins, which are many, are forgiven; for she loved much: but to whom little is forgiven, the same loveth little.

—Luke 7:41–47

∞ Keep the Right Priorities

And he spake a parable unto them, saying, The ground of a certain rich man brought forth plentifully:

And he thought within himself, saying, What shall I do, because I have no room where to bestow my fruits?

And he said, This will I do: I will pull down my barns, and build greater; and there will I bestow all my fruits and my goods.

And I will say to my soul, Soul, thou hast much goods laid up for many years; take thine ease, eat, drink, and be merry.

But God said unto him, Thou fool, this night thy soul shall be required of thee: then whose shall those things be, which thou hast provided?

So is he that layeth up treasure for himself, and is not rich toward God.

—*Luke 12:16–21*

❧ *Cut Your Losses*

He spake also this parable; A certain man had a fig tree planted in his vineyard; and he came and sought fruit thereon, and found none.

Then said he unto the dresser of his vineyard, Behold, these three years I come seeking fruit on this fig tree, and find none: cut it down; why cumbereth it the ground?

And he answering said unto him, Lord, let it alone this year also, till I shall dig about it, and dung it:

And if it bear fruit, well: and if not, then after that thou shalt cut it down.

—*Luke 13:6–9*

❧ *Ferret Out the Counter-Productive Elements*

Another parable put he forth unto them, saying, The kingdom of heaven is likened unto a man which sowed good seed in his field:

But while men slept, his enemy came and sowed tares among the wheat, and went his way.

But when the blade was sprung up, and brought forth fruit, then appeared the tares also.

So the servants of the householder came and said unto him, Sir, didst not thou sow good seed in thy field? from whence then hath it tares?

He said unto them, An enemy hath done this. The servants said unto him, Wilt thou then that we go and gather them up?

But he said, Nay; lest while ye gather up the tares, ye root up also the wheat with them.

Let both grow together until the harvest: and in the time of harvest I will say to the reapers, Gather ye together first the tares, and bind them in bundles to burn them: but gather the wheat into my barn. . . .

Then Jesus sent the multitude away, and went into the house: and his disciples came unto him, saying, Declare unto us the parable of the tares of the field.

He answered and said unto them, He that soweth the good seed is the Son of man;

The field is the world; the good seed are the children of the kingdom; but the tares are the children of the wicked one;

The enemy that sowed them is the devil; the harvest is the end of the world; and the reapers are the angels.

As therefore the tares are gathered and burned in the fire; so shall it be in the end of this world.

The Son of man shall send forth his angels, and they shall gather out of his kingdom all things that offend, and them which do iniquity;

And shall cast them into a furnace of fire: there shall be wailing and gnashing of teeth.

Then shall the righteous shine forth as the sun in the kingdom of their Father. Who hath ears to hear, let him hear.

—*Matthew 13:24–30, 36–43*

❧ Stick with the Best Product

Again, the kingdom of heaven is like unto a merchant man, seeking goodly pearls:

Who, when he had found one pearl of great price, went and sold all that he had, and bought it.

—Matthew 13:45–46

❧ Forgive

Therefore is the kingdom of heaven likened unto a certain king, which would take account of his servants.

And when he had begun to reckon, one was brought unto him, which owed him ten thousand talents.

But forasmuch as he had not to pay, his lord commanded him to be sold, and his wife, and children, and all that he had, and payment to be made.

The servant therefore fell down, and worshipped him, saying, Lord, have patience with me, and I will pay thee all.

Then the lord of that servant was moved with compassion, and loosed him, and forgave him the debt.

But the same servant went out, and found one of his fellowservants, which owed him an hundred pence: and he laid hands on him, and took him by the throat, saying, Pay me that thou owest.

And his fellowservant fell down at his feet, and besought him, saying, Have patience with me, and I will pay thee all.

And he would not: but went and cast him into prison, till he should pay the debt.

So when his fellowservants saw what was done, they were very sorry, and came and told unto their lord all that was done.

Then his lord, after that he had called him, said unto him, O thou wicked servant, I forgave thee all that debt, because thou desiredst me:

Shouldest not thou also have had compassion on thy fellowservant, even as I had pity on thee?

And his lord was wroth, and delivered him to the tormentors, till he should pay all that was due unto him.

So likewise shall my heavenly Father do also unto you, if ye from your hearts forgive not every one his brother their trespasses.

—*Matthew 18:23–35*

∾ *Listen: What Are People Demanding?*

And he said unto them, Which of you shall have a friend, and shall go unto him at midnight, and say unto him, Friend, lend me three loaves;

For a friend of mine in his journey is come to me, and I have nothing to set before him?

And he from within shall answer and say, Trouble me not: the door is now shut, and my children are with me in bed; I cannot rise and give thee.

I say unto you, Though he will not rise and give him, because he is his friend, yet because of his importunity he will rise and give him as many as he needeth.

—*Luke 11:5–8*

∽ Reach Out and Broaden Your Base

And when one of them that sat at meat with him heard these things, he said unto him, Blessed is he that shall eat bread in the kingdom of God.

Then said he unto him, A certain man made a great supper, and bade many:

And sent his servant at supper time to say to them that were bidden, Come; for all things are now ready.

And they all with one consent began to make excuse. The first said unto him, I have bought a piece of ground, and I must needs go and see it: I pray thee have me excused.

And another said, I have bought five yoke of oxen, and I go to prove them: I pray thee have me excused.

And another said, I have married a wife, and therefore I cannot come.

So that servant came, and shewed his lord these things. Then the master of the house being angry said to his servant, Go out quickly into the streets and lanes of the city, and bring in hither the poor, and the maimed, and the halt, and the blind.

And the servant said, Lord, it is done as thou hast commanded, and yet there is room.

And the lord said unto the servant, Go out into the highways and hedges, and compel them to come in, that my house may be filled.

For I say unto you, That none of those men which were bidden shall taste of my supper.

—*Luke 14:15–24*

∾ *Keep Track of Expenses*

Either what woman having ten pieces of silver, if she lose one piece, doth not light a candle, and sweep the house, and seek diligently till she find it?

And when she hath found it, she calleth her friends and her neighbours together, saying, Rejoice with me; for I have found the piece which I had lost.

Likewise, I say unto you, there is joy in the presence of the angels of God over one sinner that repenteth.

—*Luke 15:8–10*

⧜ *Act Wisely*

And he said also unto his disciples, There was a certain rich man, which had a steward; and the same was accused unto him that he had wasted his goods.

And he called him, and said unto him, How is it that I hear this of thee? give an account of thy stewardship; for thou mayest be no longer steward.

Then the steward said within himself, What shall I do? for my lord taketh away from me the stewardship: I cannot dig; to beg I am ashamed.

I am resolved what to do, that, when I am put out of the stewardship, they may receive me into their houses.

So he called every one of his lord's debtors unto him, and said unto the first, How much owest thou unto my lord?

And he said, An hundred measures of oil. And he said unto him, Take thy bill, and sit down quickly, and write fifty.

Then said he to another, And how much owest thou? And he said, An hundred measures of wheat. And he said unto him, Take thy bill, and write fourscore.

And the lord commended the unjust steward, because he had done wisely: for the children of this world are in their generation wiser than the children of light.

And I say unto you, Make to yourselves friends of the mammon of unrighteousness; that, when ye fail, they may receive you into everlasting habitations.

—Luke 16:1–9

∾ *Don't Rely on Status*

And he spake this parable unto certain which trusted in themselves that they were righteous, and despised others:

Two men went up into the temple to pray; the one a Pharisee, and the other a publican.

The Pharisee stood and prayed thus with himself, God, I thank thee, that I am not as other men are, extortioners, unjust, adulterers, or even as this publican.

I fast twice in the week, I give tithes of all that I possess.

And the publican, standing afar off, would not lift up so much as his eyes unto heaven, but smote upon his breast, saying, God be merciful to me a sinner.

I tell you, this man went down to his house justified rather than the other: for every one that exalteth himself shall be abased; and he that humbleth himself shall be exalted.

—Luke 18:9–14

∞ *Do What You Promise*

For the kingdom of heaven is like unto a man that is an householder, which went out early in the morning to hire labourers into his vineyard.

And when he had agreed with the labourers for a penny a day, he sent them into his vineyard.

And he went out about the third hour, and saw others standing idle in the marketplace,

And said unto them; Go ye also into the vineyard, and whatsoever is right I will give you. And they went their way.

Again he went out about the sixth and ninth hour, and did likewise.

And about the eleventh hour he went out, and found others standing idle, and saith unto them, Why stand ye here all the day idle?

They say unto him, Because no man hath hired us. He saith unto them, Go ye also into the vineyard; and whatsoever is right, that shall ye receive.

So when even was come, the lord of the vineyard saith unto his steward, Call the labourers, and give them their hire, beginning from the last unto the first.

And when they came that were hired about the eleventh hour, they received every man a penny.

But when the first came, they supposed that they should have received more; and they likewise received every man a penny.

And when they had received it, they murmured against the goodman of the house,

Saying, These last have wrought but one hour, and thou hast made them equal unto us, which have borne the burden and heat of the day.

But he answered one of them, and said, Friend, I do thee no wrong: didst not thou agree with me for a penny?

Take that thine is, and go thy way: I will give unto this last, even as unto thee.

Is it not lawful for me to do what I will with mine own? Is thine eye evil, because I am good?

So the last shall be first, and the first last: for many be called, but few chosen.

—*Matthew 20:1–16*